JAMES EARL CARTER:

THE MAN AND THE MYTH

JAMES EARL CARTER

The Man and the Myth

by

Peter Meyer

SHEED ANDREWS AND McMEEL, INC.
Subsidiary of Universal Press Syndicate
Kansas City

Acknowledgments

My many thanks to Philip Nobile, Tom Drape, Keith Kelleher, Lynn Cardiff, and Tim, Jane, Annabelle, Pat and Annick.

Library of Congress Cataloging in Publication Data

Meyer, Peter, 1950-
  James Earl Carter: the man and the myth.

  Includes index.
  1. United States—Politics and government—1977-
2. Carter, Jimmy, 1924-   3. Presidents—United
States—Election—1976.
E872.M49   973.926′092′4   [B]   78-21951
ISBN 0-8362-6605-6

Contents

For Marian Williams Meyer
who lived for others

Jimmy Carter and the Truth: "I'm not a liar. . . ."

"If I'm elected, at the end of four years or eight years I hope
people will say,
'You know, Jimmy Carter made a lot of mistakes, but he never
told me a lie.'"
—Jimmy Carter, May 6, 1976

If Jimmy Carter hadn't made such an issue of his personality, his glad-handing of the truth may have passed as a simple aberration to which politicians are perennially prone—a bit of exaggeration here, some selective oversight there, puff up past achievements, and downplay previous indiscretions and misjudgments. And promise everything—an inflation rate of 4 percent, jobs for everyone, government regulations written in plain English, a balanced federal budget, a reduction of taxes for middle and lower income wage-earners, an end to government secrecy, a reduction of defense spending, etc. Instead of offering a guide for the implementation of his indisputably reputable ideals, however, Carter invoked the voters to trust him.

On March 14, 1976, after Carter had already won the New Hampshire, Vermont, and Florida primaries, he was asked by syndicated columnist Robert Novak on CBS's nationally televised "Face the Nation" whether the candidate would explain how the national, comprehensive, mandatory health insurance program which he favored would be financed, how much it would cost, and whether it would be administered under private or public auspices.

"Well, I don't know the answer yet," Carter replied.

Ed Rabel of CBS News then queried Carter about "the centerpiece" of his campaign, the reorganization of the federal government. "You talk about one thousand nine hundred agencies being reorganized to two hundred," said Rabel, "and yet you really aren't willing to say which agencies are going to be eliminated."

"Well, there is no way for me to envision at this point as a full-time candidate which particular agencies in the federal government would survive three years after I'm in the White House."

By May sixth Carter had added more than fiv hundred delegate votes to his total tally, sweeping Henry Jackson out the door in an important victory in the Pennsylvania primary, and was back on television—this time with Bill Moyers—telling voters that the federal government was an "ineffective, bloated, confused, unmanageable bureaucracy." Carter promised to open up the government so that "the people could understand it and control it." He would "let the government work"; "give service to our people; . . . minimize red-tape, . . . minimize confusion, . . . minimize paperwork. . . ." He didn't mention exactly how it would be done.

"You're saying, in effect," conjectured Moyers, " 'Trust me. I will do those things.' "

"Yes," Carter replied.

"Is that right?" Moyers was rightfully skeptical. But Carter was characteristically confident.

"Yes." he said.

"And there's no question but that you have tapped a feeling in the country that wants to trust."

"Yes."

That was that. No messy specifics. No issues (who would oppose a government that "the people could understand"), but one: whether Jimmy Carter was honest and sincere and decent and trustworthy. It seemed at times as if Carter was campaigning on a platform written by Lord Baden Powell—to be trustworthy, loyal, helpful, friendly, courteous, kind, obedient, cheerful, thrifty, brave, clean and reverent. . . . on my honor I will do my best to do my duty to God and my country. . . .

Issues? "I don't give a damn about abortion or amnesty or right-to-work laws," he told one journalist. "They're impossible political issues. . . . I can't possibly help anyone—including myself—if I'm out on the edge of such volatile things, and I don't intend to be." He wasn't lying now.

According to Carter, the voters had been so "hurt and scarred" by Vietnam, Cambodia, Watergate and the CIA revelations that they wanted only "sombody they can trust—just somebody they believe they can believe." So the crux of the Carter campaign, the moral and political premise upon which he based his grueling pursuit of America's trust was his outlandishly simple promise never to lie, never to tamper with the truth.

"If I ever tell a lie, if I ever mislead you, if I ever betray a trust or a confidence, I want you to come and take me out of the White House." He said it again and again.

The statement seemed more simplistic than simple. Moyers tried to give the candidate the benefit of the doubt.

Perhaps Carter just didn't understand the nitty-gritty of Washington power politics or that the world was not everywhere such a good and decent place. "People have more doubts about your perception of reality than they do about your integrity," said Moyers.

Yes. "I understand," Carter said. He knew how bad the world was. "I see no reason for the President to lie. . . ."

And so he must have. He repeated the pledge often enough. In Baltimore, more than a year earlier, he had told a luncheon crowd that there were many things he wouldn't do to win. The list of *would-nots* was brief: (a) lie; (b) make a misleading statement; (c) betray a trust; (d) avoid a controversial issue. Five months later, in September of 1975, he rattled off the same four commandments at Florida State University. And again, a month after that, verbatim, in response to a question at a Daytona Beach rally. (He continued the litany throughout the primary campaign, though by March of 1976 he had, not so curiously, dropped *d*.)

Carter had monopolized the trust market. By doing so he gained a reputation for being an anti-politician's politician—a down-home, country born, peanut farmer from Plains (population 600), Georgia, who read the Bible each day, taught Sunday school classes and prayed twenty-five times a day as a governor. He thought himself no "better or wiser than any other person" and claimed his "greatest strength" was that he was "an ordinary man, just like all of you." Finally, a country-boy-made-good, not slick. In the end, however, Carter appeared to be not so much the ordinary man as the common ambitious politician who knew better than most the credo of his profession: "Tell me what you want to be told so that I can tell it to you." And when Jimmy Carter put his political ear to the electoral ground, he heard the rumbling of many heavy hooves beating out a message of despair over "cre-

dibility gaps" and CIA "revelations" and lying and cheating and swearing in high places, and he (being more political than most) stomped the dusty earth in reply, "I will not
ever lie." It was perhaps Carter's first broken promise.

Because he spent so much time emphasizing his "other-
ness," his distinctiveness from other politicians, his being a
large cut above the common political knavery, by claiming
that he had never lied and never would, Carter's manipulations were at the same time surprising and insuperable.*
If he seemed to be different, it was only because he was a
better used-car salesman—better at selling his solemnly
repainted, dependable, and efficient self. If a good car
could have no sawdust in the transmission, he would have
none in his. Period. If his word on the matter were im-
pugned, he would act hurt. "Ordinarily, I'm quite easy-
going and don't like to argue. When somebody insinuates
that I'm a liar, I resent it." It was a perfect tautology—you

---

*What was more surprising was how ardent Carter supporter's
could explain away their candidate's past. Professor James Baker,
for example, wrote that Carter, while campaigning for Georgia governor in 1970, "helped finance the campaign of a black running for
governor, hoping he might siphon off some of [his principal rival's]
black votes. . . . he promised if elected to invite George Wallace of
Alabama to speak to the Georgia legislature. He permitted his organization to distribute a picture of [chief rival Carl] Sanders celebrating a
basketball victory with two black Atlanta Hawks and a bottle of cham-
pagne, a fairly typical Dixie trick of the day. . . . he embraced Lester
Maddox. . . . His redneck campaign got him elected." But, as Baker
continued, Carter "could not come out for the blacks because they were
not enough to win and because coming out for them would alienate the
very poor whites who were enough to win. This was one of the am-
biguities politicians constantly face. He had to do wrong, to pretend a
racism he never felt, to do right." If true, it was curious behavior for a
man now claiming he would never mislead. But Baker and others
seemed to believe in miracles, of the political order: "Once safely
elected," he concluded, "with only the presidency above him in ambition, he could at last say the things he had felt all along." That, of
course, was Carter's instantly famous gubernatorial inauguration
phrase, "The time for racial discrimination is over."

can believe that I tell the truth because I'm not a liar—and it worked. Until standards of truth other than Jimmy Carter's own were applied.

The departure of Carter staffer Robert Shrum from the southerner's normally tight-knit and well-ordered campaign camp was the first concrete sign that Carter might be something other than the "other" he claimed to be. An experienced political speechwriter who had worked for George McGovern, Edmund Muskie, and John Lindsay, Shrum was drafted into the Carter circle by the candidate's pollster-advisor, Patrick Caddell, just before the Pennsylvania primary in April. Caddell thought highly enough of Shrum to recommend him to Carter by suggesting that "This campaign needs now at least one excellent, brilliant writer, who can pull together ideas and statements for the governor and who has good political sense. Someone who knows how to capitalize on opportunities and also how to avoid disaster."

Shrum was the first real outside standard to bump up against Jimmy Carter's touchstone. From his vantage point as a serious observer of the political stage, Shrum had been impressed by Carter—especially his sincerity and honesty—and had willingly come aboard the train that now seemed bound for the presidential nomination. On board, however, Shrum was immediately shocked as he listened to the Southern Baptist say of Maynard Jackson, he "can kiss my ass," or "I don't want any more statements on the Middle East or Lebanon. Henry Jackson has all the Jews anyway. . . . we get the Christians." After less than ten days, Shrum had had enough and quit, bitter and disillusioned.

"What made it hard," he told Washington *Post* reporter Jules Witcover, "was to listen to the stump speech: 'I will never lie to you; I will never mislead you,' said with fervor and passion, and seeing people believe it." Shrum had broken through the Carter tautology. What he had seen inside the circle was a different Jimmy Carter than the one visible from outside, the one mesmerizing voters—as he had apparently hypnotized himself—with continual repetition of his mantra, "I'm not a liar . . . I'm not a liar . . . I'm not a liar. I have no sawdust in my transmission." For Shrum the contradiction was serious: The most important issue of the campaign had been blown away. Carter was dishonest and insincere.

Shrum accused Carter of concealing his true positions on many issues. He had, for example, publicly promised to cut defense spending by 5 to 7 percent; but in private, according to Shrum, he admitted that he "might favor a substantial increase." (In fact, as President, Carter did increase the defense budget.)

He also would not support a plan to make miners automatically eligible for black-lung disease benefits after thirty years work for reasons that he would hardly have admitted in public. "The plan is too radical," Carter told Shrum. "I couldn't endorse these things. They are too controversial and expensive. It would offend the operators. And why should I do this for Arnold Miller [president of the United Mine Workers] if he won't come and endorse me? I don't think the benefits should be automatic. They *chose* to be miners."

(Though Carter later denied all of Shrum's quotations, saying the speechwriter had "dreamed up eight or ten conversations that never took place," the candidate proved himself to be a president totally capable of the cynical attitude Shrum reported him expressing toward the miners' plight. When Carter's Council of Economic Advisors, in May of 1978, ordered that federal rules designed to protect some eight hundred thousand cotton industry workers from the ravages of brown lung disease not be implemented, CEA chairman Charles L. Schultze reasoned that in light of Carter's (recent?) concern about inflation, "it is important to insure that any new regulations do not impose unnecessary or uneconomic costs on American industry." Ten months earlier Carter had shown little more concern for poor women when he justified a suspension of federal funds for abortion by saying, "Well, as you know there are many things in life that are not fair.")

As jolting as Shrum's revelations may have been to those who had come to believe Carter, it wasn't necessary to wait for word from the inside to document the deceptions.

In keeping with his famed rural origins, the candidate enjoyed his humble lies—even those spoken in less than humble locales. At a posh reception in Los Angeles in the summer of 1976 given for Carter by actor Warren Beatty, he took the opportunity to speak of the responsibilities the rich had for the poor. Among the fifty-odd superstar guests at the Beverly Wilshire Hotel listening to the candidate explain why he and other elected officials should not cater to the likes of Cadillac and Rolls Royce owners were Carroll O'Connor, Louise Lasser, Sidney Poitier, Faye Dunaway, Paul Simon, Diana Ross, Robert Altman, James Caan, and George Peppard. If they took offense at Carter's forthright pledge as a public servant to "bypass the big shots, including you and people like you," they could find solace in his admission that he too was once like them, and understand his championing of the less fortunate because he lived among them.

"In the county where I farm," said Carter, talking about what he knew best, "we don't have a doctor, we don't have a dentist, we don't have a pharmacist, we don't have a registered nurse; and people who live there who are very poor have no access to health care." A pitiful situation, one that needed rectification by anyone's standards, even those of "big shots" and reformed big shots. What no one in the audience knew, however (unless, of course, they had been to the tiny county in Georgia where Carter Farms Inc. owned more than two thousand acres of land or phoned the Southwest Georgia Health Systems Agency), was that Carter had gotten carried away by hyperbole. Instead of no doctors in Sumter county, there were twenty-one active ones; instead of no dentists, there were eleven; instead of no pharmacists, sixteen; and in all, there were one hundred seventy-seven active registered nurses instead of none at all.

While Carter could whittle away at the medical, legal, and teaching professions—as he did that day in Los Angeles—he tried to finesse as much political leverage as possible out of his brief associations with professionalism. In many of his campaign speeches he proudly announced that he was—*inter multa alia*—"an engineer" and a "nuclear physicist." In fact, he was neither. His only degree was the Bachelor of Science he received from the Naval Academy at Annapolis in 1946 where there was no course on nuclear science. As a naval officer, he said he "studied special graduate courses in reactor technology and nuclear physics at Union College" while assigned to the Atomic Energy Commission's Division of Reactor Development at Schenectady, New York.

Did that experience qualify Carter as a nuclear engineer? (The Carter camp reluctantly gave up the "physicist" label after being challenged, explaining that "It's a matter of semantics whether you regard there being an important difference between the two words.") Hardly. He took the "special graduate courses" for only one semester and, according to one of the professors who taught in the program, "No one who took that program could be classed as a nuclear engineer—it was at quite an elementary level." One professor of engineering wrote a letter to *Science* magazine expressing his dismay that the "credentials of those who call themselves engineers are not very carefully examined." "To call oneself a 'professional engineer,'" he pointed out, "in any of the fifty states or the District of Columbia, a person must complete an eight-year training program" and pass "a professional-level examination lasting two days."

Like many of the broad themes in the Carter stump speeches—honesty, decency, efficiency in government, morality in foreign affairs—the deceptions were repeated with disconcerting frequency. Even in the White House, Carter would still refer to himself on occasion as a nuclear physicist.

Or, when asked why he constantly referred to his address "to" the United Nations even though, as New York *Times* reporter James Wooten pointed out, Carter "knew he was referring to a speech he had made before an international energy conference that had nothing to do with the United Nations other than it happened to be meeting there," the candidate would say, "Oh, did I say 'to.' Well, I meant to say 'at.'" Nonetheless, Carter "to"-ed again.

He would also stump from audience to audience telling them that while governor of Georgia he had "achieved welfare reform by opening up one hundred thirty-six day-care centers for the retarded and using welfare mothers to staff them. Instead of being on welfare, these thousands of women now have jobs and self-respect." The problem was that no such program involving welfare mothers existed. "If Carter ever mentioned such a program," press aide Jody Powell told journalist Steven Brill, "I guess he was mistaken." But Brill said he heard Carter "make the same mistake" five times in three days.

The Carter people didn't always do such a good job denying their candidate's tampering with the facts. Instead, they often compounded the deception, lending credence to a belief that they weren't credible by misleading a second time in order to disclaim the original lie. When

Brill suggested in a 1976 *Harper's* magazine article that a speech Carter had given for George Wallace Appreciation Day in Red Level, Alabama, in 1972, had been omitted from the Georgia archives because of gubernatorial (i.e., Carter) censorship, Jody Powell denied it. Brill's point, of course, was that Carter had a reason for not wanting the speech made part of the archives: concealing his previous ties with the segregationist Wallace. (By that time, Carter himself was contemplating a move into the national political arena.) Powell claimed that no transcript of the speech existed. And responding to Brill's implication that Carter was closer to Wallace as governor than he was admitting as presidential candidate, Powell said that in examining local press accounts one would find that the only reason Carter made the speech was to "wish Wallace a speedy recovery" from the wounds suffered at the hands of Arthur Bremer. When Miami *Herald* reporter Phil Gailey checked up on Powell's source, however, he found that the Dotham (Alabama) *Eagle* had written an account of Carter's appearance quite different than the one Powell said the paper gave. "Although Carter stayed away from specifically endorsing Wallace," read the *Eagle*'s report, "he emphasized forcibly many of the stands the Alabama governor had taken in his bid for the Democratic presidential nomination."

Powell was even more misleading when trying to minimize the implications of a Carter statement that Brill *did* discover in the archives. In a 1972 letter to a Mrs. Dempsey of Alabama, Carter wrote that he had "never had anything but the highest praise for Governor Wallace. . . . I think you will find that . . . Governor Wallace and I are in close agreement on most issues." What was interesting was Powell's response: "The letter to Mrs. Dempsey was written by a staffer, never seen by Governor Carter, and did not accurately express his views. . . . Had the writer of the article asked, he would have been told of the three-letter-initial code used to identify staff letters." What Gailey discovered, however, was that the "code" letters on the Dempsey letter were those of Jody Powell himself, Carter's most trusted aide.

Carter and his Georgia campaign contingent seemed so infected by the consuming ambition to gain the White House that they refused to believe that there was anything in Carter's past to be ashamed of—or anything that really couldn't be turned to advantage. Their political sensibilities, their reading of the popular sentiment, was astute. Too astute, perhaps. So well did they understand the desires of the voters (at least that small majority of the electorate that finally chose Jimmy Carter instead of Gerald Ford) that they bestowed on Carter talents and achievements that were not always his. They seemed intent on fleshing out the skeleton of the perfect politician; resurrecting from the dung-heap of politics an ideal man. They were hell-bent on winning the election.

The details of campaign rhetoric were lost in some larger vision. Ends justified means as much as they seemed to dictate them. And the deceptions perpetrated in the service of those ends were dismissed as unimportant— nit-picking, they told the critics, semantics.

There seemed to be no maliciousness in the deception. But the absence of any malice of forethought was justification in retrospect. Carter's pledge "never to *deliberately* mislead you" was an escape hatch of sorts. He hadn't "ever *deliberately* hurt one of my opponents," he said. "I *try* not to. I *don't remember* when I have. There *may have been* something. . . ." If someone could prove that Jimmy Carter lied, would he quit the campaign? "I think I would, because I haven't told a lie." (Translation: Sincerity is its own justification.) Would he resign the White House if proved a liar? "Well, I can't say that. But there will be times when I'm asked a question that I might refuse to answer. But if I give an answer, it will be the truth." (Translation: if . . . maybe . . . well . . . but . . . I'm sincere . . . .) Carter was an honorable man, but one more faithful to the ideal image of himself than to reality. Trying sincerely to fulfill that ideal was the same, it seemed, as actually having achieved it. And if he were there—so the unspoken logic continued—the process of arriving must have been the right one.

That logic was most evident as he enunciated one of the most fundamental promises of his campaign: "If you don't want me to reorganize the federal government, don't vote for me."

The biggest obstacle, however, was getting people to believe that he could actually carry it off. He was not a politician with any experience in governing on a national scale. He was only a one-term governor of a state with fewer than five million people and smaller revenues than the city of New York. If he were to change a federal government that he so often called "bloated," inefficient, incompetent, obsessed with secrecy, he would have to prove that he was capable of mastering a bureaucracy that dwarfed in every way his tiny Georgia enclave.

And he was not known, as his media adviser Gerald Rafshoon told him in 1972 when he was first considering the presidency, for his "heavyweight ideas and programs." So the first priority in campaigning for the White House, suggested Rafshoon, would be the formulation of "a heavyweight program" and projection of "a heavyweight image." Carter would have "to convince the press, public and politicians that he knows how to run a government (he has a record to prove this)." Even though Carter had been a governor less than two years, his advisers were already telling him what his accomplishments were, how to utilize his "record." "We could relate the accomplishments of your administration," Hamilton Jordan told him in his famous 1972 strategy memo, "to the theme that revitalized state government is the key to solving many of the problems in this country. . . . The thrust of your national press effort should be that state government is working in Georgia. . . ." Before he had even proven that he could effectively manage state government, Carter was running for president as a man capable of making government work. He had a "reputation" before he had a record. The scenario was written long before the events which it described had occurred.

It wasn't surprising, then, to read much later in a Carter for President brochure: "As governor, Jimmy Carter pushed through a hard-nosed reorganization of the state's overgrown bureaucracy. He eliminated 278 of the 300 agencies and slashed administrative costs by 50 percent." Voters could be justifiably awed by such a tale of managerial wizardry. "How did he do it?" was more a deferential statement of respect than a question. Maybe he could, after all, eliminate one thousand seven hundred of one thousand nine hundred federal agencies, eliminate red tape and paperwork and inefficiency and confusion and make it all work again.

Maybe he could. But the fact was, he didn't do what he said he did in Georgia. If the bureaucracy was "overgrown" when he assumed control of it, what was it when he left? The state's total budget increased more than 58 percent during the Carter administration. Its outstanding debt increased by almost 25 percent (to $1.09 billion). Its total per capita tax collections grew by 51 percent, four points more than the national average. And instead of a decrease in the number of state employees (excluding teachers), their ranks were enlarged by more than eight thousand.

As for "slashing administrative costs by 50 percent"—in *Why Not The Best* he had "slashed" them "more than half"—Carter was saying more than he knew. The Georgia state auditor Ernest Davis wasn't "able to identify any savings that resulted from reorganization per se," and Carter spokesman Rex Granum, after being questioned by reporters, admitted that the figure was "just an estimate." In his autobiography Carter said he left office with a state surplus of "almost two hundred million dollars," but later corrected the figure downward to one hundred sixteen million.* But this huge surplus assumed less mythic proportions when it was realized that everything else on the ledger sheet increased (the total budget, the debt, revenues) and that Carter had inherited a one hundred million dollar surplus upon taking office.

Technically, of course, Carter did exactly what he said he did—he "reorganized," regrouped, reshuffled, revamped a perhaps "overgrown" bureaucracy. But the clear implication was that reorganization had meant less government. "I ran on a platform promising reorganization of the state government," he recounted in his autobiography, "stating that there were one hundred forty-six agencies in all. Our later analysis revealed three hundred, and we abolished two hundred seventy-eight of them!" In fact, there never were three hundred state agencies. There were hundreds of boards, bureaus, and commissions that existed only on paper or received no state funds—and Carter did eliminate some two hundred forty of these paper agencies. But even those that were technically part of the Georgia government—there were sixty-five budgeted agencies—were not so much "abolished!" as

---

*Press Secretary Powell later explained the discrepancy by saying that the two-hundred-million-dollar figure was "the working estimate of surplus," the only available figure at Carter's disposal when he "began work on the book." Not surprisingly, however, Carter didn't bother to inform the readers that his figure was only an estimate, nor did he change the numbers in subsequent printings.

moved around. In the end, he compressed the sixty-five into thirty (not twenty-two as he so often claimed), creating super-agencies like the new Department of Human Resources which brought together all agencies relating to public health, welfare, and vocational rehabilitation, or the Department of Natural Resources, a conglomeration of thirty-three separate agencies and their bureaus. (Many critics doubted even the advantages of the shuffle. As Georgia's commissioner of labor, Sam Caldwell, rebutted, "There may have been a few inconsequential boards that were eliminated, but mostly he just created a monster, like HEW in Washington.") Carter was also forced to drop his campaign statement that as governor he had eliminated two thousand one hundred unnecessary state jobs. The state auditor again corrected the record, pointing out that the two thousand one hundred jobs existed on paper only.

As was his wont, Carter stated a generalized fact (e.g., reorganization), that while indisputable and laudatory, was also meaningless unless bolstered by an example. And as also was his wont, he discovered examples that were, at best, gross exaggerations of fact.

In his headlong pursuit of power he perennially imparted the misleading impression (buttressed by distorted and deceptive "facts") that he had already thwarted one bloated bureaucracy (in Georgia) and that he would do the same upon his arrival in Washington. It appeared that the common assumption—as Carter cultivated the image of an outsider who would clean up the mess in the federal bureaucracy, "bring the growth of Government under control," and eliminate 90 percent of its agencies—was that Carter was anti-big-government. That assumption, however, proved to be as false as the premise upon which it was grounded (i.e., the Georgia record). One early example of that was a report released by Carter's Office of Management and Budget which recommended job ceilings for the following year (1978). For almost every department OMB suggested an increase in the numbers of full-time, permanent, civilian federal employees: a total net increase of five thousand in one year. And that was before the Department of Energy stepped into the arena, or a new Department of Education was proposed. Another example was Carter's federal pay-raise recommendation in October of 1977. Even though estimates had shown that in 1976 the average federal employee earned more than sixteen thousand dollars annually—almost five thousand dollars more than the average private-sector employee, and that not counting the generally more lucrative pension plans, provisions for earlier retirement and exclusion from payment of social security taxes enjoyed by the federal worker—the president approved an across-the-board 7 percent pay raise that would cost the taxpayers an additional three billion dollars. All symbolic gestures to the contrary—such as his announcement in his "fireside chat" eight months before: "We have eliminated expensive and unnecessary luxuries, such as door-to-door limousine service for many top officials. . . . Government officials can't be sensitive to your problems if we are living like royalty here in Washington"—the thirty-ninth president showed little willingness to do anything more drastic with big-government than rearrange the chairs.

A New York *Times*/CBS News poll conducted in late October asked whether the president or congress "pays more attention to what people like you think" and found that 42 percent of the public said congress; 40 percent thought it was the president. Could the president restore trust in government? In January, 70 percent of the public had said yes; in October, a scant 51 percent thought he could.

And the irony in all the Carter talk about his reorganization record in Georgia was that it came within the context of his promise to bring back to Washington "a government

that can be trusted"; a government that would be led by a
president who would reveal "immediately" any instances of
"error or malfeasance," who would "speak with a clear
voice," and "set a standard of morals and decency and
openness."

> I can't imagine somebody like Thomas Jefferson tiptoeing
> through a minefield on the technicalities of the law, and then
> bragging about being clean afterwards.
> —Jimmy Carter, May 4, 1974

Jimmy Carter was not very pleased to see the news
splashed in banner headlines across the front page of the
Washington *Post*: CIA PAID MILLIONS TO JORDAN'S
KING HUSSEIN. His presidential administration was less
than two months old. He worried that the news would
disrupt Secretary of State Vance's meeting with the King.
The secretary was due to land in Jordan that same day for
sensitive talks on prospects for Middle East peace. It might
blow the whole thing, damage hopes for a settlement, and
infuriate Hussein, who for years had been a loyal ally.
Hussein had been receiving millions of dollars yearly, said
the *Post,* in a program that dated from early in the second
Eisenhower Administration. The story quoted unnamed
CIA officials who said that project "No Beef" was little
short of "bribery." "Hussein has a well-publicized taste for
sports cars and airplanes," Carter read, ". . . the CIA has
provided Hussein with female companions [and] body-
guards for [his] children when they were abroad in
school."

There was also reason to worry because it was the *Post*
that decided to publish; and the reporter investigating was
a man world-famous before anyone outside Georgia had
heard of Jimmy Carter—Bob Woodward. (Richard Nixon
would remember well.) The story would receive a great
deal of attention. It was only February 18, 1977, and al-

ready Carter was stuck with a flap over the pernicious CIA, ironically, one of the targets of his campaign attacks on government secrecy.

Senator Charles Mathias had gotten wind of the *Post* investigation just the week before and passed the word on to Carter. On February sixteenth, the president summoned *Post* executive editor Benjamin Bradlee and reporter Woodward to the White House, and at that unusual meeting let the two know that he preferred that the story not be published. He explained to the newsmen that he himself had only learned of the payments to Hussein at the same time he had heard of the *Post* investigation, and had immediately ordered that the payments be stopped. If the paper wouldn't kill the article, would it at least delay publication in the interests of Mid-East peace. Bradlee—a confidant of one president, a bitter enemy of another, and not awed by the executive aura—would agree only to give Carter twenty-four hours notice before publishing Woodward's account. A few hours after the meeting Carter was informed that the Hussein story would be on the streets that Friday, the eighteenth.

The President declined to comment on the veracity of the *Post* story. It was the "administration's policy not to comment on—either to confirm or deny—any stories concerning alleged covert activities," said Jody Powell at a press briefing on Friday. But the following Tuesday the president called congressional leaders together for a closed-door meeting to confirm the fact that Hussein had received the money and that Carter had withdrawn it. Reports of the meeting were leaked to the press.

Then, at a press conference two days later, Carter announced that he had "adopted a policy . . . of not commenting directly on any specific CIA activity." He would say nothing more than that he had studied the "more controversial revelations" and found that some were "quite erroneous," and others had "some degree of accuracy."

But he assured the public that he had "not found anything illegal or improper." He made no mention of stopping the payments.

Despite the initial front page fascination exhibited by the Washington *Post* and the national media, the King Hussein/CIA episode was notable more for its revelations about President Jimmy Carter than its exposé of the U.S. spy agency. Carter exhibited with what ease he could turn a simple mistake into a confusing deception. First, after letting it be known that he had stopped the payments to Hussein, implicitly conceding that something was not right, he turned around and proclaimed that there was nothing even "improper" about them. In early March Hussein asserted that he had not been informed of any plug in the flow of dollars, but his statement could not be verified because by this time the Carter administration had a "policy . . . of not commenting on any specific CIA activity."

In the process of getting elected Carter had promised that "if the CIA ever makes a mistake, I will call a press conference and tell the people." Instead of calling a press conference, however, he tried to squash the story. Carter must have known he was in a no-win situation: the *Post* was going to "tell the people," and Jimmy Carter, who already knew the story but hadn't told, would be caught with his credibility pants wrapped around his ankles. He cut the payments to Hussein to protect himself and then tried to bargain for time with Bradlee, still hoping, perhaps, that Vance would exit Jordan so that he could reveal the story himself, thereby saving both the Mid-East talks and face at home.

Bradlee, however, by this time, held all of the cards. And not only did he refuse to give Carter the necessary time, but he insulted the president by publishing the story at the very moment that Vance was to meet with Hussein.

At that point Carter began to confound his no-win position. Rather than admit that, yes, he had known about the payments but didn't reveal them because of Vance's trip, and say a few *mea culpa*'s, he instead enmeshed himself in further deception. First, he called a secret meeting with the congressmen (hardly a respectable way to reveal anything). Then he apparently changed his mind about the propriety of the payments themselves, said the CIA had made no mistake (though still hedging: *some* of the "controversial revelations" *did have* "some degree of accuracy"), and ended (after the whole affair had become sufficiently muddled) by closing the information lid on everything. It was a perfect lesson in the Carterization of Aristotelian logic: If *A* (if the CIA makes a mistake . . .), then *B* (then I will . . . tell the people); but if not-*B* (if I've already not told the people), then not-*A* (then there were no CIA mistakes).

Carter was a wizard at "tiptoeing through a minefield on the technicalities," and a master of both the humble lie (similar to what Robert Shrum called the "technical truth"*) and the ornately decorated grand deception. In

---

*In the June 11, 1976, issue of *New Times* magazine Shrum offered this succinct analysis of how the Carter wizardry could be used: "Carter is on record as favoring a 5 to 7 percent reduction of defense spending. The pledge had brought some important liberals to his campaign. The possibility of another technical truth: Carter has never identified the base figure for the cuts; as president, he could cut 5 to 7 percent from the Ford trendline budget for 1978. Spending could rise by billions, but Carter could insist he kept his word. Not the spirit perhaps, but the words."

As it happened, Carter turned Shrum into something of a political Isaiah. In January of 1978, just after Carter unveiled the first complete budget of his eleven-month old administration, Michael Ruby and Rich Thomas filed this report for *Newsweek* magazine: "Even though his 'prudent and tight' Defense Department outlays would rise by $10 billion, [Carter] conceded last week that a 9.5 percent increase would still be 'consistent with campaign pledges to the American people.' How so? The $117.8 billion defense budget is $5 billion less than what Ford had projected for fiscal '79—a year after Carter's pledge."

the campaign he had often dredged up the CIA as an example of both the absence of morality in the conduct of foreign affairs and the diseased condition of a government which not only tolerated but advocated secrecy and lying. Carter pledged "to strip away secrecy of government." And it sounded very good, decent and moral during the campaign to promise that CIA transgressions would be immediately and publicly revealed. But that promise was made when other people were sinning and not 'fessing up.' The voters may have believed that somehow Carter as president would remain as unattached to the nefarious institutions that had made the mistakes as he was as a candidate; believed that probably those groups would continue to lie and cheat, but that Carter would now be there to expose them. The problem, however, was that Carter himself had promised not to sin or lie or mislead or cheat and to assume as well total responsibility for the actions of agencies under his control. "The president ought to be personally responsible for everything that goes on in the executive branch of government. . . ." He had painted himself into a difficult corner. The CIA was *his* as president, part of the promise, another Carter appendage pledged to honesty.

As his long-time Georgia friend and adviser Charles Kirbo once remarked, "There are two things that Jimmy Carter hates. He hates making a mistake and he hates admitting it." The only way out of the corner is to paint a door on the wall and pretend that it opens. If it doesn't, pretend that the paint is dry. If it isn't, pretend that it didn't stain your shoes. If it did, turn off the lights.

That was something of what Carter did with the Washington *Post* story. Eight months later he tried again.

At a presidential news conference on September 29, 1977, a reporter asked Carter how he was going about making a decision on how to handle the perjury case of former CIA director Richard Helms. It was pointed out that Attorney General Bell at one time had promised to seek the president's counsel on the matter.

"He has not consulted with me," replied the president, "nor given me any advice on the Helms question. I am familiar with it through the reading in the press .... I think he will make a report to me and possibly a recommendation fairly soon. But until this moment, he has not yet done so."

False. On November first the attorney general set the record straight. He revealed that, in fact, he *had* met with Carter to discuss the Helms case on July twenty-fifth, just two months before the President denied having consulted with him. It must have been more than a spontaneous encounter. Bell brought two key aides with him and Carter called in the vice-president and the national security adviser Brzezinski. The reason that Bell even mentioned the July twenty-fifth meeting at his November first news conference was to emphasize the fact that the Justice Department's decision to plea-bargain with Helms had not been made lightly (one suspects that he didn't bring it up in order to tag his president a liar). All of the significant issues were touched upon on July twenty-fifth, said Bell, including whether the intelligence community was subject to the same laws as other Americans, how the case would affect future congressional inquiries of intelligence matters, what national security risks were at stake, etc.

"We weighed the factors which I thought were involved," Bell said later. "We were satisfied from our study to date that it was possible to prosecute. We were authorized by the president to determine the possibility and feasibility of plea-bargaining and to keep him advised of any developments in this matter."

Why would Carter have lied about the meeting? It was doubtful that it simply slipped his mind. He, after all, had requested it, and by the testimony of his own attorney general, it had been a crucial meeting in the process of disposing of the Helms case—Carter himself advising Bell to see if copping a plea wasn't a possible solution. Even had Bell not told on Carter, however, it would have been almost impossible to believe Carter's September twenty-ninth suggestion that he knew of the "Helms question" only "through reading in the press." The case was too important to Carter.

First of all, it represented the first significant test of Carter's repeated campaign vow "to end once and for all a double standard of justice. I see no reason why big-shot crooks should go free and the poor ones go to jail." Helms had many friends and sympathizers in high places—both before and after being accused of perjuring himself in front of a congressional committee. They included W. Averell Harriman, former New York governor, ambassador to Russia, confidant and adviser to presidents Kennedy and Johnson; former vice-president Nelson Rockefeller; CBS commentator Eric Sevareid; *Time* magazine Washington bureau chief Hugh Sidey; and Carter's own secretary of energy, James Schlesinger. And if well-heeled friends were not enough, Helms himself had all the right credentials for being classed as a "big-shot": He had studied in Switzerland and Germany, graduated from Williams College in 1935, worked for United Press (even scooping an interview with Adoph Hitler), was a lieutenant commander in the Navy attached to the Office of Strategic Services (OSS) during World War II, stayed in the spy business (which was quite respectable at the time), rose through the ranks of the CIA, became its director in 1966, and capped his career with an ambassadorship in 1973. Given Helms' stature, it would seem odd indeed that a president (especially one who made so much political hay by campaigning against a government that would let the big-shots off the judicial hook) wouldn't bother to inform himself of the case other than by "reading in the press."

The second reason why Carter's feigned innocence struck such a hollow chord was the case itself. It was while the Senate Foreign Relations Committee was considering Helms' nomination as ambassador to Iran in 1973 that his difficulties began. At those hearings the former CIA director testified that his agency had not secretly channeled money into Chile in an attempt to subvert the presidency of socialist Salvador Allende Gossens. But in fact, more than eight million had gone into such an effort; and seven months after Helms' original false testimony, on September 11, 1973, Allende was killed in a bloody coup, ending forty-six years of civilian rule in Chile and toppling the world's first freely elected Marxist government.

As congressional committees pushed for more information about America's involvement, it became apparent that Chile had long been an arena for important CIA covert operations with far-reaching implications for the American intelligence establishment. It was disclosed that the giant multi-national communications company ITT had offered Helms one million dollars to further subversive activities in order to protect its Chilean telephone company from nationalization; which, if true, would mean that ITT had later perjured itself in order to collect ninety-four million dollars in insurance payments—from a U.S. government agency—after its Chilean holdings were nationalized. William Colby, Helms' successor as chief spy, testified that Chile was an experiment in the technique of using large sums of cash to bring down a government: It was believed that some twenty million dollars had been spent in Chile since 1964. Other disclosures revealed the Nixon administration's involvement. Henry Kissinger, Nixon's national security adviser (confirmed as secretary of state ten days after the Chilean coup), had authorized the

expenditure of at least the eight million dollars which
flowed into the country between 1970 and 1973. Helms'
role was crucial, and prosecuting him for perjury brought
with it the possibility of revealing not only the full extent of
U.S. manipulations in Chile, but also a vast network of
subterfuge involving top government officials and business
executives.

For those that believed in the type of covert operations
conducted in Chile and the necessity to protect the information about the logistics of the operation, letting Richard
Helms plea-bargain was the least that could be done to
safeguard the "national security." "It is a shame that Dick
Helms should have been in court at all," said energy czar
Schlesinger after the former CIA director pleaded *nolo
contendere* to two misdemeanor counts and received a two
thousand dollar fine and suspended jail sentence. "It
would have been a national disgrace had the outcome been
more severe. He should treat the outcome like a dueling
scar—it underscores his service to his country." But Carter hadn't chosen Schlesinger to lead the Energy Department because of his views on national security and government secrecy.

But neither had the voters chosen Carter as president
because of his support of CIA adventurism abroad. In
fact, Candidate Carter had given the impression that he
was wholly opposed to such un-American things as over-
throwing freely elected governments abroad. The CIA
had been a repeated target of his morality spears during
the presidential campaign, ranking with Vietnam, Cambodia, and Watergate as a buzz word for what was most
wrong with America. "Our government has pursued dubious tactics, and the phrase 'national security' has sometimes been a cover-up for unnecessary scandals and for
unnecessary secrecy," he told the B'nai B'rith delegates in
September of 1976. "We stumbled into the quagmires of

Vietnam and Cambodia, and we carried out heavy-handed efforts to destroy an elected government in Chile." But the forceful language of an ambitious and astute presidential candidate often becomes a mockery of itself in a cautious and conciliatory president. One year and twenty one days after B'nai B'rith, though nothing had changed the facts of the "heavy-handed efforts to destroy an elected government in Chile" and not a word of Richard Helms' perjured testimony of 1973 had been removed from the public record, President Carter claimed he was "familiar with [the Helms question] through reading in the press," making a point to emphasize his ignorance of the case as if he had only heard of it yesterday: *"I have no way to know yet* the strength of the possible indictment or charges. *I have no way to know yet* the seriousness of the offense with which he will be charged [may be charged, says the White House Press Office clarification]. And *I have no way to know yet* the seriousness of possible damage to our own national security if massive revelations of intelligence techniques and documents are made either to ourselves or to our friends and allies." [Emphasis added.] Carter had unlearned quite a bit in a year. On November 10, 1978, he was still trying to pass Helms off to someone else: "The Helms case is one that we *inherited. I've never met Mr. Helms.* I don't believe the attorney general has ever met Mr. Helms. This is a serious problem that *evolved in years past.*" [Emphasis added.] But it wasn't that Jimmy Carter had inherited Richard Helms so much as the CIA had inherited another president.

Even though his turnabout on the Helms case was less volte-face than change of masks, Carter must have known that his plea-bargaining with Helms was another "national security . . . cover-up for unnecessary scandals," and a renunciation of his high-principled ideals. It was a dilemma for Carter that he seemed to believe could be solved by fabrication. It was a dilemma that to a great extent flowed from the fact that Carter was, as Stanley Hoffmann, professor of government and chairman of the Center for European Studies at Harvard, pointed out, "a man who operates at two very different levels, with missing links between the two. One is the level of high principles, noble yet sometimes fuzzy. The other is the level of daily pragmatic politics, flexible (almost dazzlingly so) and minutely detailed." In foreign policy, said Hoffmann, writing almost a full year into the Carter administration, the "missing links" created a "strategic vacuum" which in turn led to "traumas of execution." "When there is nothing between disembodied, if appealing, goals, and the level of daily execution, an outside observer all too easily gets the impression of watching a rudderless ship."

It was something of a "trauma of execution" that Carter suffered from on September twenty-ninth when he answered a straightforward question about Richard Helms by (falsely) pleading ignorance. Again (as in the Hussein episode or the Georgia record distortions), Carter must have known that he was caught in a self-made *Catch-22:* stuck between his rock of principle and his hard place of contradictory past action (or inaction); between his "disembodied, if appealing, goals"—in this case, to clamp down on the "big shots" and "justify the character and moral principles of the American people"—and the policy he had already suggested that his attorney general pursue. But instead of trying to understand or explain the contradiction, he tried to protect himself from it, claiming with a forced and awkward and outrageous untruth that (despite everything that the Helms case represented) Bell had "not consulted with me, nor given me any advice." (Possibility of a "technical truth": Perhaps it was *Carter* who had consulted with Bell, and it was thus true that Bell had not consulted with Carter? Perhaps, too, Bell had not really given *"advice,"* only counsel? Perhaps the President only asked questions of Bell, and so Bell didn't really *give* as much as relinquish. Perhaps. Perhaps. In fact, Carter's eventual explanation was not quite so absurd; but almost.)

How would a man who "hates making a mistake and hates admitting it" free himself from the deception? Apparently, by enlarging it, muddling it with technicalities. After telling one reporter at a November tenth news conference that "a public official does not have a right to lie," Carter fielded a question about why he had denied consulting Bell when, in fact, he had spoken with the attorney general on July twenty-fifth. Carter artfully sidestepped the question by implying that the July twenty-fifth discussion wasn't important enough to remember:

"The September twenty-fifth [the president meant July twenty-fifth, says the official White House transcript] meeting was not . . . a thorough discussion of the Helms case. It was a briefing . . . There was a general discussion there, fairly brief."

(Carter, later in the same response, even admitted talking to Bell on another occasion about the Helms case [he had evidently prepared himself for this question], but it was "one day in passing.")

Even more curious than Carter's "brief-encounter" explanation—which was still at odds with everything that Bell had said about the meeting—was his considerable restatement of the original September twenty-ninth exchange. The following is the full text of New York *Times* reporter Charles Mohr's question and the president's own November tenth (free) translation:

September 29:
Mohr: Mr. President, Admiral Turner of the CIA did a speech this week at Annapolis in which he said that the attorney general would have to make a decision as

November 10:
The President: The question that was raised in September was based on a statement by Admiral Turner, who heads up the CIA, the national intelligence commu-

to whether it would further the national interests to prosecute the case of Mr. Richard Helms, or whether it would be better to waive the case in order to save secrets. But the attorney general said that he was going to consult you on this.

I wonder if you can tell us your views on how you are reaching this decision as to whether certain material should be declassified for a possible trial in this case?

The President: He has not consulted with me, nor given me any advice on the Helms questions.

nity, that we were faced with a prospect of two alternatives: One was a decision not to prosecute at all, and the other alternative that Admiral Turner mentioned, which was in the reporter's question, (sic) that the complete trial would be held with the revelation of national security secrets.

(no deletions)

I replied that the attorney general had never presented that information to me, which was true.

The president seemed bottled up by either self-delusion or an exaggerated case of retrospective wishful thinking, or both. Did he really believe that "he has not consulted with me, nor given me any advice" was the same as he "had never presented that information to me"? Carter may have *wished* that he had given the latter response on September twenty-ninth; but he hadn't, so he simply said he had.

Jimmy Carter would have to learn that the truth resided somewhere outside of himself. It was not his alone to tinker with, to mold and manipulate according to some self-appointed ambition, however noble or sincere or righteous or self-effacing he believed his ambition to be. This is what *actually* transpired on September twenty-ninth, Carter was saying on November 10. So he rephrased with remarkable accuracy (again, a testament to his preparation) the statement upon which Mohr had based his query, chose to ignore Mohr's actual question, and then restated ("I replied . . . ") his response with total inaccuracy. Bill Moyers had hinted at the problem almost twenty months before. "People," he told Carter, "have more doubts about your perception of reality than they do about

your integrity." Was there such a thing as an honorable
liar?

Richard Nixon had had his Alexander Butterfield, in
charge of "internal security" at the White House, to trot
before the public a tape-recorded truth that was the thirty-
seventh President's eventual undoing: "Nixon bugged
himself." And the evidence against Nixon was there, in his
own words, finally. For everyone to see, it was Nixon recoil-
ing upon himself, a public (it had been only private before)
self-immolation. But when the hypocrisy moved beyond
Nixon, the "internal security" unburdened of its secrets, it
became undeniable, the contradiction too blatant to deny
for almost everyone but the man caught up in it.

Jimmy Carter was his own Alexander Butterfield. He
bugged himself in public. There were many leaks in his
internal security and no Plumbers to plug them. He was
not as tricky as Tricky Dick; hadn't really learned to
temper the tendency toward public self-destruction in the
fires of paranoia. Nixon fought off the contradictions because he believed that no one was on his side and he was
ultimately a survivor. Carter ignored them because he
thought God was on his side and in the end it wasn't all that
important to survive. Nixon was an alley-fighter and a
lawyer and he said, "I'm not a crook." Carter was a
crusader and a minister and he said, "I'm not a liar." Had
Carter been more the street-wise politician he wouldn't
have rushed so fecklessly into his lie. After all, Mohr
hadn't even asked Carter if he had consulted with Bell,
only "how you are reaching this decision." But so anxious
was he to protect his image as a man out to bring justice to
the big shots and openness and honesty to government
that he rushed to disassociate himself from the deal his
Justice Department was making with Helms. "Oh, what a
tangled web we weave," wrote New York *Times* columnist
William Safire about the affair. "I'll never lie to you,' said

candidate Jimmy Carter, again and again and again. The matter that troubles those who hope he will be a successful one-term president is not so much whether he is lying to us, but whether he is lying to himself."

"I was taught that just staying narrowly within the law is not enough. Just staying within the law will never be enough for a Carter campaign or a Carter administration."
                              —Jimmy Carter, December 12, 1974
"I think I have good judgment. I think I know something about people. I've watched them succeed and I've watched them fail, and I've seen all the in-betweens."
        —Bert Lance, quoted by Robert Shogan, *Promises to Keep*

There was talk that the affair might be the undoing of the president. Headline writers had another scandal on their hands and were lavishly squeezing doomsday ink into boldface type: "Can Carter Survive Lance?" "The Unraveling of the Carter Presidency." "Carter's Broken Lance." And the inevitable, "Lancegate." The ghost of Richard Nixon and all the president's men was uncannily reappearing. Money, politics, and power had once again joined forces to weave a complicated tangle of alleged influence peddling, fraud, fabrication and cover-up. Even die-hard skeptics of conspiracy theories couldn't avoid the threads of mutual concern that linked financiers to lawyers to high level presidential appointees to friends of the president to Jimmy Carter himself. At the center of the web was Thomas Bertram Lance, Carter's friend, personal banker, fellow Georgian and political appointee, standing closer to the center of power than any other. He was the first hired. He was also the first "fired." And throughout, even as he accepted Lance's resignation, Carter would admit to nothing improper.

The Lance affair began—though only a few close Carter associates knew—in the span of a few short weeks just after Jimmy Carter was elected. The word was out in mid-November that the president-elect would bring to Washington his long-time friend Bert Lance, president of the National Bank of Georgia. On November twenty-second, Lance paid a visit to the office of the regional director of the Comptroller of the Currency in Atlanta, Mr. Donald Tarleton. A few hours later Tarleton gave the order to rescind a cease and desist order against Lance's bank. On December first Lance lawyer Sidney Smith—a member of an Atlanta law firm headed by Philip Alston, Carter's later choice for ambassador to Australia—called the United States attorney in Atlanta, John Stokes. The next day, Stokes called off a Justice Department investigation of Mr. Lance. And the day after that, December third, Jimmy Carter nominated Bert Lance as director of the Office of Management and Budget. It was not until eleven months later, on the day that Bert Lance left office under a cloud of suspicion and with numerous government bodies investigating him, that Carter admitted—incorrectly, his press secretary claimed later—he knew of both the comptroller's disciplinary agreement with Lance and the Justice Department's criminal investigation.

The Lance affair—so dubbed by Alexander Cockburn and James Ridgeway in the *Village Voice* less than two weeks after the Senate confirmed the nomination—not only brought out the worst in Jimmy Carter and his new administration, it sabotaged the best. It confirmed for many of his long-time critics and borderline sympathizers that he was a man of limited vision, inexperienced in the ways of running a country, incapable of seeing his way through the tug and pull of power politics in Washington. It all but extinguished Carter's most hallowed flame: his honesty and integrity. Carter made a crucial mistake in December of 1976. He either failed to inform himself of Lance's banking indiscretions, a sign of sloppy screening for a position of such importance. Or, if he were aware of the suspicious wheeling and dealing of his friend and the two government investigations which it spawned, he failed to inform the public. In either case, Carter committed himself to a grand deception.

"Once a cover-up strategy is decided upon," wrote William Safire, a former speechwriter for Richard Nixon and the man who won a Pulitzer prize for his New York *Times* columns detailing Lance's transgressions, "the subsequent tactical decisions are choices between greater and lesser mistakes." What was most intriguing about the Lance affair was not whether the swashbuckling Georgia banker was a crook—though that question was being pursued by the Department of Justice—or an unethical banker—though that was eventually doubted by almost no one except Jimmy Carter and Lance himself and was, in fact, made a formal charge by the Securities and Exchange Commission and the Comptroller of the Currency in the spring of 1978—but why, with a president who promised "immediate" revelation of "errors or malfeasance," it took almost nine months and constant prodding to locate even the tip of Bert Lance's beguiling iceberg.

The beginning of the end for Bert Lance as chief banker of the nation didn't come until six months into the new administration. Not surprisingly, Lance was the cause of his own demise. In mid-July, 1977, at the budget director's request, President Carter sent a letter to the Senate Governmental Affairs Committee (the same that had originally given speedy approval to the appointment) asking that Lance be allowed to forego the promise to divest himself of his controlling interest in the National Bank of Georgia, the state's fifth largest financial institution. (In the ethical flush of the *interregnum* President-elect Carter had promised that his appointees would not only live by the letter of the conflict-of-interest law, but would avoid even the "appearance" of a compromising connection.) The White

House explained that the public imposition of the December 31, 1977, deadline for the sale of the stock had artificially depressed the market value of Lance's shares and thus Lance, in short, would lose his shirt if he had to sell (or if not his shirt, at least a million dollars or so). The request didn't seem too outrageous to the committee. After all, Carter had set such high conflict-of-interest standards for his cabinet that a slight exception for the president's most valued aide could be made. In this case, however, the exception was the fact that the letter was a deception. What the president didn't mention—the letter was drafted by Lance and fellow Georgian and White House counsel Robert Lipshutz—was that the stock of NBG had dropped precipitously from over fourteen dollars to less than nine dollars, not because of Carter's super-ethics but because of Lance's questionable ones. The boomerang always comes back. Lance had so over-extended himself and NBG during his tenure as its president with risky financial deals that his successor, Robert Guyton, was forced to rein in, write off some $2.3 million in bad real estate loans and cancel the quarterly dividend. That was a fact that the man who had swept so casually through senate confirmation could ill afford to reveal. So he didn't, and the senate seemed willing to move favorably on Carter's request.

Unfortunately for Lance and Carter, however, they got "blindsided," as William Safire, the one who did the blind-siding, immodestly pointed out. The New York *Times* columnist had gotten wind of a dubious loan that Lance had negotiated just two weeks before his senate confirmation, and in a July twenty-first column went about throwing spears at Lance's "financial house of cards." He sketched a suspicious portrait of the budget chief as a peddler of political influence in exchange for financial gain; his major source of collateral being proximity to Jimmy Carter.

On January 6, 1977, Lance borrowed $3.4 million from one of the nation's largest banks, the First National of Chicago (whose president, J. Robert Abboud, by coincidence, perhaps, was a Democrat of power and prestige in the windy city and a former college roommate of John Moore, Carter's "ethics" adviser, a member of Philip Alston's law firm, and later the president's choice to head the Export-Import Bank). Safire claimed that the terms of the loan were so good that it had to be a "sweetheart loan." To have the director of OMB in hock by that amount— especially when it was known that Lance had ambitions on the Federal Reserve chairmanship—should have been worth something. As was later revealed it was worth enough to defer interest payments and demand no collateral on $1.6 million of the total: not an arrangement offered to just anyone and possibly a transaction in violation of banking law.

And the reason Lance needed the Chicago money was to pay off a previous loan of $2.7 million from Manufacturers Hanover Trust in New York, which money he had used in purchasing his controlling interest in the National Bank of Georgia in Atlanta in 1975. But the MHT loan also smelled a little "sweet." Just after the New York deal, on June 19, 1975, Lance had whisked his friend, former Georgia governor and presidential candidate, Jimmy Carter, up to New York for a courtesy call on one of the bank officers who had arranged the Lance loan. Additional collateral, perhaps? It surely wouldn't have hurt to drop Carter's name around to build confidence in a credit risk, and then produce the man himself to prove, at least, your political worth. But helpful though it may have been in securing the loan, it wasn't enough to pay the premiums. Lance had promised the New York bank additional collateral in the form of stock dividends from NBG; but rather than paying up, he took fourteen thousand shares paid to him at the end of 1975 and used them as collateral on yet another loan, this one from Chemical Bank, also in New York. No wonder, then, that Lance received numerous dunning letters from MHT until First National of Chicago came to bail him out.

Revelation of those kinds of dubious banking shenanigans was not the hoped-for fruit of Carter's request to the Governmental Affairs Committee. And to further complicate the administration's "cover-up" difficulties, on the same day that Safire's article sent heads wagging, Treasury Secretary Michael Blumenthal (neither a member of the "Georgia Mafia" nor a great admirerer of Lance) was instructing his comptroller of the currency to hurry along his investigation of Mr. Lance's past banking practices, an inquiry that had only been *reopened* (the circumstances surrounding the abrupt termination of the previous comptroller order against Lance had not yet been revealed) a week before.

While the comptroller was assuring three different congressional committees that a report would be forthcoming, the press, led by Safire, continued to trot more shady financial ghosts out of Lance's closet: his bank had deposited two hundred thousand dollars in a non-interest bearing account at First National of Chicago only a few months before Lance received his personal $3.5 million; the Central States Teamsters had deposited its eighteen-million-dollar pension fund in Lance's bank during the heat of the presidential primary campaign, even though, up to that time, NBG had never had an account of over two million dollars for its tiny three-man trust department to handle; Lance, after becoming OMB chief, arranged a meeting with Secretary of the Treasury Blumenthal for two Tennessee banking brothers—Jake and C. H. Butcher—to which banks he was in hock by some four hundred forty-three thousand dollars; two months before Lance brought

Carter to New York for the June nineteenth meeting at MHT, the candidate had borrowed seven hundred eight thousand dollars from Lance's bank (NBG had also given Carter's Warehouse, Inc., a $2.4 million loan during the 1976 election year, double the normal line of credit enjoyed previously by the Carter business).

At the very least, it became evident that Lance had violated the Carter code of ethics and conflicts-of-interest that had been announced with such fanfare the previous January: "It will be the policy of the Carter-Mondale administration to appoint . . . only persons of high ability who will carry out their official duties without fear or favor and with an equal hand, unfettered by any actual or apparent conflicts of interest." It seemed more than a simple irony that just two days after the code was unveiled on January 4, 1977, Bert Lance, soon-to-be Carter's most powerful cabinet member, became a $3.4 million debtor to a powerful private financial institution which must have known that, as one senate investigator later remarked, at the time "Lance was, in fact, drowning in debt." Also ironic was Carter's choice as the nation's banker a man who seemed much more adept at juggling other people's assets and playing one debt against another than at balancing books. The house of cards was beginning to topple, but the jovial banker from Georgia and his political benefactor, the President of the United States, were scrambling to deny that such a house even existed, *ever* existed.

When the comptroller released his four-hundred-three page report—after only a month of inquiry—on August eighteenth, Lance summoned the press, got Carter to fly in from Camp David to be at his side, and the two breathed a joint sigh of relief that finally the president's friend had been vindicated. Carter, who said he personally studied the report, was effusive with praise for Lance, "a man of complete integrity" who continued to enjoy the president's "complete confidence and support. . . . Bert, I'm proud of you." The President seemed to have taken leave of his senses. Was he proud of the more than fifty irregularities, "unsafe and unsound banking practices," the suggestion that some matters be turned over to the Justice Department because of possible criminal violations, and a number of "open matters" which the comptroller was going to pursue—all of which was contained in the report. "President Carter's fond remark was one of those human ad libs that defies rational planning," said Safire. Even some of Carter's advisers were amazed at the president's unfettered denial of the damning evidence presented by the comptroller. "They [the Georgia contingent] never bothered to check with anyone who could have warned them that some of the judgments would never wash," said one. "They thought they'd have two days of bad press and the thing would be over." More skeptical observers saw more in the president's actions (not only at the press conference, but also the deceptive letter to the senate committee the month before) than a temporary aberration of political judgment or an isolated mistake. "President Carter and his men did not act as bumblers or innocents in this affair," said Safire. "The seeming 'mistakes' in handling its development were only less-evil choices forced upon them; once the decision was made to allow the Lance train to leave the station in November 1976, nearly everything that flowed from that decision was inexorable." Carter had subtly changed the rules of the game because he had struck out already. His pious pledge to avoid *even* the appearance of impropriety had become a strategy to protect at all costs *only* the appearance of integrity and pay no heed to its substance.

By the summer of 1977 it had become too late to admit that Carter probably knew more than he told. Or that some members of the transition team had been aware, before the Lance appointment was announced, of the Georgia banker's questionable past banking practices— like trading interest-free deposits by the National Bank of Georgia for personal loans, allowing large overdrafts by his family, the unethical and possible illegal use of collateral due to one bank in order to obtain a loan from another, the use of a bank plane for private excursions— knew about the comptroller's squelched order and the abruptly suspended Justice Department investigation, and concealed information from congressional committees. Even as the facts of the "cover-up"—as it was then being called—began to dribble out in late August, the president seemed to stand above it all, at no time aware that anything had been concealed from anyone.

Donald Tarleton, the regional director of the comptroller's office who rescinded the enforcement agreement against Lance's Calhoun First National Bank moments after the visit from Lance on November twenty-second, curiously couldn't recall "if the papers drifted to the top of the work pile on my desk, or if Mr. Lance's visit served as a reminder." His superior in Washington, Acting Comptroller Robert Bloom, though at first angered by Tarleton's move (he understood its implications?), quickly decided to fall in line. He withheld details of the report from the FBI, said nothing of the overdrafts to the senate committee, and told the senators that Lance was "well qualified." Only months later did he admit that he had told Lance he wanted the job of Comptroller of the Currency. "Put yourself back in time," explained Bloom. "It's two days before the inauguration. Mr. Lance was Mr. Carter's first appointment. It was well known that he was his close personal friend. Nobody likes to be a skunk at a garden party."

How many possible garden party skunks were there in the Lance cover-up? The president made a tentative attempt in early September to deny that he or his aides had done anything smacking of impropriety: "If there are any people who worked in the transition time who made an inquiry about Mr. Lance's affairs, they did it without my knowledge and without my authority, and it would have been contrary to my expectations." It was a weak defense, part of which was sufficiently rebuffed in the later congressional testimony: some of the Carter people *had* made inquiries.

They knew about the Justice Department's criminal investigation into the possible illegal use of corporate airplanes—including trips to college football games, the Mardi Gras, and Warm Springs, Georgia, to watch his friend kick off the presidential campaign—one of which Lance had sold to the bank after becoming its president for a nifty forty-thousand-dollar profit to himself. The federal attorney in Atlanta called the FBI off the Lance case on December second, a day after speaking with Lance's lawyer Sidney Smith on the phone, the day before Carter formally (it had already been widely reported that Carter would name Lance to the budget position) announced Lance's appointment. That information didn't reach the senate committee; neither did an FBI report on Lance which summarized some of the material and was passed on to Carter aides.

The revelations were very interesting—and damaging to the carefully cultivated Carter administration image of strict probity beyond the narrow confines of legal technicalities. Even John Moore, Carter's "ethics" adviser during the transition, a member of Philip Alston's Atlanta law firm (as was Sidney Smith) and later appointed by Carter to head the Export-Import bank, knew; but couldn't remember if he had told the president-elect. Everyone seemed to know about the terminated comptroller's order and Justice Department investigation except Carter.

Then, inexplicably, one month after his "without-my-knowledge . . . without-my-authority" hedge, Carter came clean, admitting that he was a potential skunk at his own garden party. On September twenty-first, after his near-tearful opening statement explaining the resignation of "a good and honorable man," the president was asked when *he* first knew about the charges against Lance. "The first time I heard about it [the overdrafts from Calhoun National Bank]," he explained, "was when Bert mentioned it to me in Plains about two weeks later—I think the date now determined to be the first of December. I was called from Atlanta and told that the matter had been resolved by the comptroller's office and by the Justice Department." What the president had admitted was that he had known that a prospective cabinet nominee was under criminal investigation, and knew that that investigation would be dropped the day before it was officially terminated.

Jody Powell, the ever-vigilant presidential press secretary, who was immediately aware of the dangerous implications in Carter's admission, tried the next day to correct the president's recollection, arguing that his boss was really only made aware of the "problems in the comptroller's office" on December first: he "misspoke" himself when he said "Justice Department."

The explanation, however, seemed extremely weak. It was widely known that Jimmy Carter had a mind that absorbed and retained and enjoyed the smallest of detail (in his autobiography he recalled such things as losing "twenty-two pounds (down to one-hundred thirty)" in his futile first campaign for governor, and personally shaking hands "with more than six-hundred-thousand people" in his victorious 1970 race; or at a Democratic pre-convention soirée that journalist Richard Reeves attended, Carter proved his astounding memory when he cwlled to a large black woman, "Mazie, the last time we talked, you didn't have to stand in line like this." "Mazie Woodruff,"

Reeves remarked, "a grandmother thirteen times and a candidate for county commissioner back home in North Carolina, was thrilled that the candidate had remembered her. They had met only once before—in Winston-Salem in March . . ."). And it thus seemed rather unlikely that Carter, having characteristically recalled the exact date of his conversation with Lance, would somehow blur the extremely crucial fact of whether his future budget director was, only two days before the announcement, telling him for the "first time" about a Treasury Department inquiry or a criminal investigation by the Justice Department. It was also evident at Carter's Wednesday's press conference that his mention of the Justice Department was more than a simple slip of the tongue (a Freudian slip, perhaps, because in the political cover-up game, Carter *should not have* said what he did) or an innocent misstatement, because Carter pressed on, invoking twice more the name of Justice: "On that date," he continued, "was the first time that either Bert or I knew that the Justice Department had been involved at all. And my understanding then was that it was an oversight and had the oversight not occurred that the Justice Department would have resolved the issue long before."

The president's own recantation (like Powell's) was not unexpected, though the timing was tinged with irony. At his next press conference, on September twenty-ninth, after reassuring Charles Mohr of the New York *Times* that he had never consulted with Attorney General Bell on the Richard Helms case (which happened to be untrue), Carter fielded a delicate question from Martin Schram of *Newsday:* "Who told the truth about Lance and the criminal investigation? You on September twenty-first, or Jody Powell on September twenty-second?"

The President. I don't recall. [oops! Not yet, Jimmy, not yet.] I did say that in the last press conference. And when

Jody asked me about it afterwards, I told him I was mistaken. [Okay, now, the total amnesia.] I don't recall at all ever knowing that the Justice Department itself was involved in the Bert Lance overdraft or other problems last year.

Carter was back on track—after a brief flirtation with what some thought was the truth. "I believe that Jimmy Carter," said Safire, "—too upset by the forced resignation of his friend to stick to the cover-up script—told the truth in his press conference [of September twenty-first]. In his own unforgettable phrase: 'I don't think any mistake was made.'" But it was too late to change the script. It had been written, as Safire often pointed out, at the moment when Carter and his aides chose to conceal Bert Lance's warts with a good ole Southern bear hug of camaraderie. After December 1, 1976, the Carter team was committed to the double standard.

There was no need to search far for historical parallels. While Carter was still campaigning, Lewis Lapham at *Harper's* observed the candidate's penchant for telling lies that "were so easily found out" and "was reminded of Nixon repeatedly announcing his innocence to smaller and smaller audiences." As the Lance affair unfolded with Carter becoming an increasingly awkward defender of an increasingly obvious deception, Richard Nixon's White House became an appropriate metaphor for the machinations of the Georgia team. Press Secretary Jody Powell tried to plant damaging allegations against Charles Percy (ranking Republican member of the Senate Governmental Affairs Committee who had suggested that Lance resign) in several newspapers after digging through FBI files, claiming that the senator had unethically used Bell and Howell's corporate aircraft while he was president of the company. Powell's "dirty trick" was exposed when one of the papers discovered that Bell and Howell never owned an airplane. *Time* magazine's president-watcher and cautious Carter supporter, Hugh Sidey, pointed out that "Powell . . . turned out to have some of the Machiavellian instincts of Nixon's Ziegler—and about the same skill." Garry Wills, a Nixon scholar (*Nixon Agonistes*) and seasoned political journalist, was less reserved: "Attacks on Lance were taken as attacks on Carter. Jody Powell Ron-Zieglered serious questions into a mockery of 'third-rate-burglary' responses when he discounted the story of half-million-dollar overdrafts, juggled accounts, and reusable collateral." "Even Richard Nixon," said Doug Ireland in *New York* magazine, "was never so stupid as to name Bebe Rebozo his budget director."

But Carter persisted, right through to the day that Lance tendered his resignation (and beyond), echoing, even then, if only in less strident and obvious tones, the old Nixonian hounded-out-of-office theme song: Bert had done nothing wrong, he simply couldn't carry out all his OMB duties with the many unproved allegations floating around; and besides that, Bert had to go home to clear up some pressing financial matters that resulted from the sacrifices he made when he became a public servant.

Carter would not admit that the "high standard" of conduct he piously enunciated at the beginning of his administration was for Bert Lance quite a different standard; that Lance's honesty and integrity had more to do with "tiptoeing through a minefield on the technicalities of the law"—the strategy he condemned the Watergate culprits for employing—than with avoiding "impropriety" or even the "appearance of impropriety." Carter changed course in the middle of the stream, but he pretended all the while to be paddling into the glorious sunset of vindication. "Just staying within the law will never be enough for a Carter administration," he once said. But for Lance toeing to the letter of the law was plenty. It was a good trick: defending Lance as if he were in a court of law, subject to the rules of evidence demanded in a criminal proceding, and then exonerating him "completely" because he had been convicted of no crime. Lance's much ballyhooed nationally televised senate testimony just prior to his September twenty-first resignation was not presented in a court of law, but Carter acted as if it were. The president believed that if "Bert could not answer the allegations adequately" (were the Nielsen ratings his barometer of "adequate"?), at the senate hearings, then *that* would somehow be "proof" that he "violated the law." But, said Carter, "That was not the case." And so he had quite ingenuously given the senate the responsibility of proving Lance a criminal—which was not, nor could it be, their task—and then claimed vindication when it hadn't. Case closed. To the reporter who tried to focus in on the inconsistency by pointing out that even the comptroller had said that the multiple bank overdrafts Lance used to finance his Georgia gubernatorial campaign were a violation of federal banking statutes, Carter retorted, "You're trying to succeed where the Senate Committee failed. There was no judgment made that Bert Lance did anything illegal." Not yet.

At the September twenty-first resignation news conference, the president said repeatedly that Lance's "honesty and integrity have been proven." But, in fact, nothing to that point had been "proven" except that Lance seemed to be a pretty shady character. The August eighteenth comptroller's report—as damaging as it was—made it clear that the Lance investigation was far from complete; a federal grand jury was empaneled (in Atlanta) in November to see whether Lance should be prosecuted for criminal violations of the law. By the end of December six different federal agencies—the Justice Department, the Securities and Exchange Commission, the Comptroller of the Currency, the IRS, the Federal Deposit Insurance Corporation, and the Federal Election Commission—were all pursuing Bert Lance investigations and it soon became known that even as budget chief—despite promises to the senate confirmation committee that he would engage in no private banking activities—he gave advice to two men on the takeover of a large Washington, D.C. banking holding company.

On January 20, 1978, Carter traveled to Atlanta to lock arms with his old friend at a five-hundred-dollar-a-plate fundraiser hosted by Lance as if presidential favor would have no impact on a grand jury then trying to decide if Lance might be a criminal. (Not so curiously, when it was a question of making even a simple statement about the case of the Wilmington Ten, Carter had a much different feeling about presidential responsibility *vis a vis* the judicial process: "There is a very strict prohibition, as you know," he demurred the previous June, "against the encroachment of the Executive Branch of government on the Judicial Branch." But Carter was not a president to Bert Lance, he was a loyal friend, come hell or high indebtedness; and friendship was not *just*, it was compassionate, warts, conflicts-of-interest, overdrafts and all. The only mistake Ben Chavis and the nine other defendants in North Carolina had apparently made was not being a friend of Jimmy Carter.) Lance retained his White House pass and was a welcome house guest. He travelled to foreign countries, calling himself a "special envoy of the president," with diplomatic passport X-000065. All this while being investigated by numerous federal agencies and negotiating another ambitious and questionable bank takeover. All this despite Carter's conflict-of-interest pledge "to ensure that former government officials cannot use their personal contacts gained in public service for private benefit." Lance continued to work both sides of the street, both sides of the

Atlantic; Carter continuing to lend (demanding no collateral) Lance the prestige of presidential favor.

On February seventeenth, the Washington, D.C. company, with which Lance became intimately familiar while budget director, Financial General Bankshares (FGE), filed a civil suit against Lance, charging that he had illegally conspired with a number of others to take control of the company. A month later, the S.E.C., which was already in the midst of an investigation into Lance's Georgia banking practices, filed similar charges against Lance, four wealthy Arabs, three well-connected American entrepreneurs, and a Pakistani-born financier. For a man who the president said was resigning from the OMB because "he needs to go home and take care of his own business," Lance very quickly involved himself with a lot of non-Georgians.

Together the defendants seemed to represent a potential plague of bubonic conflict-of-interest, influence peddling and international intrigue, irrespective of their intentions on FGB, the $2.2 billion bank holding company headquartered in Washington. Some of their curricula vitae read like a script of characters from *All the President's Men:*

—Bert Lance: Described by *Newsweek* magazine as "perhaps the most trusted all-purpose adviser to a president since Robert Kennedy." A former budget director of the U.S. who still sees the president regularly and carries a special-privilege passport which assures him unimpeded entrance to foreign countries. Lance is a self-made millionaire who knows the banking business inside and out.

—Agha Hasan Abedi: A Pakistani, Abedi is president of the London-based Bank of Credit and Commerce International. BCCI is 24 percent-owned by Bank of America, the world's largest financial institution. Acted as the intermediary in Bert Lance's National Bank of Georgia stock sale to Saudi Arabian millionaire Ghaith R. Pharaon; and hired Lance as a consultant to BCCI less than a month after he resigned his OMB cabinet post. He arranged for substantial personal loans to Lance. Abedi also runs Systematics Inc, a data processing service company for banks that is 80 percent controlled by Stephens Inc., the nation's tenth largest brokerage firm.

—Jackson Stephens: Owns the controlling interest in Stephens Inc. and is, according to the Washington *Post,* "one of the country's wealthiest individuals," with "investments in banks, gas reserves, coal fields and insurance companies." Over the previous few years Stephens developed a political and business friendship with Lance, who *reintroduced* him to Jimmy Carter (a classmate of Stephens' at the Naval Academy). Is a prominent political fundraiser, supporter of President Carter, and a member of the executive committee of the Democractic National Committee.

—J.W. Middendorf 2nd: President of Financial General Bankshares and a former Secretary of the Navy. The S.E.C. suit claimed that Lance had met with Middendorf in April of 1977, three months after Lance was confirmed as head of OMB, to "assist Middendorf in assembling a group to purchase the FGB stock."

—Eugene J. Metzger: A Washington, D.C., lawyer, formerly employed by the office of the Comptroller of the Currency. Legal counsel for FGB as well as a major stockholder. His law firm offered a job to former Acting Comptroller Robert Bloom, the man who okayed the cancellation of the controversial cease and desist order against the National Bank of Georgia just after learning that Lance was to be Carter's Budget director.

—Sheik Kamal Adham: Former head of Saudi Arabian intelligence.

—Sheik Sultan Bin Zaid al-Nahyan: Ruler of Abu Dhabi and President of the United Arab Emirates, whose per capita income is almost three-thousand dollars more a year than in the United States. UAE is a prominent member of the Organization of Petroleum Exporting Countries.

Bert Lance had a difficult time staying out of trouble. Because of the well-publicized and continuing warm relationship between the former budget director and the president, the S.E.C. suit, in itself of little momentous import, made all too obvious Lance's agility at skimming across the political waters like a well-thrown stone. His gaming strategy was the same after the disgrace of resignation as it had been before: play all over the board, fast and loose, with well-chosen pieces. Not that Lance wasn't a pawn himself, even if a willing one. His co-defendants were men of immense financial and political prowess in their own right; but none of them were as close to the center of power as Bert Lance was—and remained. None were considered Jimmy Carter's "brother." If Agha Abedi, who was responsible for bringing the two sheikhs into the "conspiracy," needed a consultant on international financial matters, why turn to Bert Lance, a former president of a local Georgia bank which had only three people working in an international department that was less than two years old? Why hire Bert Lance and pay off his million dollar loans, when a principal stockholder of your company is the world's largest and most experienced financial institution with hundreds of international experts who only expected a good Christmas bonus from their employer? The answer seemed obvious enough. "Mr. Lance's wealthy new friends from the Middle East may well be under the impression that they are buying, along with the stock, a degree of access to political power in this country," commented the Washington *Post*. The financial stratosphere liked, if it could get it, contact with stratospheric politics. Big money likes to keep company with big politics.

While Bert Lance himself was a little short on the big money (almost five million dollars in debt when he left OMB), he was long on big politics and the grandiose finagle. He knew people, knew how to barter with them and cajole them and succeed like the scrappy haggler at an Arabian bazaar. "I think I know something about people," he boasted. Politics was Bert Lance's game. Not elective politics, it was too public: he lost in his one venture into it, to succeed Jimmy Carter as governor of Georgia, in part because he exposed himself as a high-roller, worth over three-million dollars he said, and was fatally dubbed by his opponent "Loophole Lance." Government constrained him. It demanded too much playing by the rules and, especially because of the odorous residue left by the lawless Nixonian street fighters, it eventually spurned the man who bent the rules to his own selfish ambitions.

Bert Lance also knew, most importantly, Jimmy Carter. Carter was a man who seemed to be everything that Lance was not: a man who was rigid and unspontaneous and hated the unknown; who hated inefficiency and incompetence; who decried the nation that had "no understandable purpose, no clearly defined goals, and no organizational mechanism to develop or achieve these purposes" (underline "purpose," "defined," "goals," "organizational," "mechanism" and "achieve"); who was tight with his money and his morals; who believed that uncertainty was "a devastating affliction in private life and in government." And Bert Lance was everything that Carter was not. He was as flexible, volatile, and spacious as Carter was constrained. What the hell was wrong with taking the bank plane to Mardi Gras or Warm Springs? There had been some business purpose in all those excursions, said Lance. And he was probably right. Bert Lance was always doing business, everywhere wheeling and dealing. Why, asked

Senator Ribicoff the week before the resignation, citing a bank examiner's report which stated that Lance had violated banking laws in 1971 by giving excessive loans to bank officers—why did Lance previously testify that bank examiners had "never" accused him of violating banking law? "Senator," replied Lance, "when I said 'never,' I was referring to the years 1972 to 1977." There was no rule that Lance couldn't slide by. He was loose. Forget the technicalities, just concentrate on good ole Bert, an honest and decent man.

That's what Jimmy Carter did in his own fashion. Carter was an assiduous planner; he organized his world with meticulous care; he was a master technician. He didn't enjoy bumbling or unexpected change or mistakes; and he squirmed and squirmed to avoid admitting that he had made a mistake, that he had somehow deviated from one of the many narrow little paths in his well-ordered world. When he was bumped out of the Georgia gubernatorial race in 1966, he fell into a deep depression. "I was going through a state in my life then that was a very difficult one . . . Everything I did was not gratifying. When I succeeded in something, it was a horrible experience for me." He hated to lose, hated to be pushed off the course that he had chosen. It took a spiritual conversion to get back on track, a "rebirth" to give him confidence again and the courage to stay the course. Did he or did he not know about the Justice Department investigation on December 1, 1976? Of course he didn't. He "misspoke" himself when he mentioned "Justice Department." He had chosen Lance and he had supported him and proclaimed his confidence in him for ten months, and he wasn't going to change now. "I think Lance was qualified then; I think he is qualified now." As different as the two men were, they had entwined themselves in the same deception.

If Carter was tied to Lance because of his narrowly constricted view of friendship and the need to remain faithful to it, Lance continued to trade on that friendship because his expansive view allowed for few conflcts of interest. Carter himself provided the appropriate and ironic symbol for their relationship when he tagged his old friend to be a representative of the "Friendship Force," a people-to-people group founded by Carter to promote good-will throughout the world. And there was Bert Lance, in early March 1978, a deposed Budget Director of the United States, a subject of numerous federal investigations, giving a deposition to lawyers in his current brush with the law about his possibly illegal conspiratorial connections with millionaire bankers and former spies from Saudi Arabia and Crown Princes of Abu Dhabi and high-powered political fundraisers, when he announces that he has an appointment to keep. And off toots Bert Lance to the White House for lunch with the president. "He wasn't able to come back [for more depositions] the next day," explained the Washington *Post,* becuase, as his lawyer explained it to the judge, he was off on a ten-day trip for "a series of meetings with heads of state in Europe in connection with . . . the Friendship Force." When he returned, the president invited businessmen to lunch at the White House where they would hear Lance report on "a ten-nation European visit with heads of state." Curiously enough, as *Time* magazine, pointed out, "Lance had visited only five countries and met no heads of state."

Carter and his White House had closed themselves in an ever-shrinking box where denial and verbal gymnastics alternated as tools for escape. They had moved slowly and subtly away from such unabashedly futile claims as the President's August eighteenth declaration, "I have reviewed the report of the comptroller . . . and my faith in the character and competence of Bert Lance has been reconfirmed. I see no other conclusion that can be drawn . . ."

By resignation day, the president had become lawyerly and cautious (except for his startling confession that he knew of the quashed criminal investigation), still defending Lance's integrity but now it was because there was no "proof" that his friend had ever done "anything improper at all, that he's violated any law." The president was trying now to extricate himself from the "case" while still stalking the moral high-road: "Bert Lance is my friend. I know him personally as well as if he was my own brother. I know him without any doubt in my mind or heart to be a good and honorable man." But Carter was really only playing the part of priest at the gallows. What was interesting was what Carter chose *not to know* about his "brother": "I don't know the details of Bert's financial dealings back home; I don't have the time nor the inclination to learn them. All I know about it is what I have had a chance to read in the news media." (Problem: The entire Lance affair revolved around *nothing but* "Bert's financial dealings back home." How then was Carter able to make such positive statements about the propriety or legality of Lance's actions or call some press reports "exaggerated," "unfair," and "untrue," if all he knew was what he read in the news media. Was one to assume that in the face of his biggest domestic crisis, with some critics accusing him of obstruction of justice and calling for a special prosecutor, the president relied totally on newspaper reports for his information? At least Carter was consistent in the manner he chose to try to avoid getting trapped in an embarrassing deception. With the Richard Helms case as well, he was "familiar with it through reading in the press.") Some things he knew; others he ignored. It was an epistemology of convenience, the art of selective forgetfulness. While appearing to remain loyal to his *friend*, he removed himself from the *case*, the details, the issues, basing his support on at once more constrained and more amorphous grounds.

By April of 1978, the White House was defending Lance (as it had to in order to remain consistent) in the most innocent way possible. In a story entitled "The Ostracism of Bert Lance: The White House asks him to fade away," *Time* magazine reported on an hour-plus meeting between Lance and Hamilton Jordan in which "Jordan told Lance that he was embarrassing Carter, even endangering his presidency" and suggested that he "keep as much distance as possible between himself and the president." Jordan denied the story with a neat defense of Lance that, like Carter's earlier brotherly love—lawyerly ignorance support, was no defense at all. "He's our friend," said Jordan. "It's not been demonstrated that he's done anything illegal or wrong in his personal life."

The Georgia team was preparing for Lance's inevitable fall, drawing the wagons tightly around the last tiny scratch of ground that remained defensible: friendship is no crime. Neatly forgotten by the White House were its "high standards of ethics," its promise to avoid even the "appearance of impropriety"; forget the canceled criminal investigation, unethical bank overdrafts, "sweetheart loans," cover-ups and obstructions of justice. The president had squeaked through the affair, admitting nothing (except for his retracted admission that he knew everything), constantly retreating until he found the moral high ground of brotherly love. He bowed to the obvious signs of political patronage: Lance turned in his diplomatic passport. He allowed Lance to retain his White House pass: a simple and harmless (according to the White House) gesture of friendship. For the rest, for the "affair" itself, the former budget director was on his own.

On April twelfth Lance stepped in front of the delegates to the American Society of Newspaper Editors convention in Washington to bemoan the treatment he had received at the hands of the press, telling his attentive audience that

he was a "case study in current press practices." He up-
braided the media for the many instances of "careless, erroneous or biased reporting." "Nobody believes anybody
anymore." And he warned the assembled representatives
of the Fourth Estate that if they didn't clean up their act
and start exercising "self-discipline and internal reform,
other groups may find it necessary to step in and subject
the press to the same rigorous standards of ethics and
truthfulness that the press applies to the rest of us. That
threat is called censorship . . . "

If the newspaper executives gave Lance a healthy round
of applause, it may have been because they remembered
something that Lance had apparently forgotten; that "the
rigorous standards of ethics and truthfulness" which
brought him down were those of his friend Jimmy Carter;
that the press only reported Carter's promise to bring to
Washington "only persons of high ability" who were "unfettered by any actual or apparent conflict of interest";
that it was the president who boasted of "the extraordinary
standards that we have tried to set in government."

Less than a week after Lance's lashing of the press, New
York *Times* columnist Safire was awarded a Pultizer prize in
journalism for his early-warning series of revealing articles
on Lance: a back-handed response to Lance's condemnation of the press.

On April twenty-sixth came another response as two federal agencies finally weighed in against Lance. Both the
Comptroller of the Currency and the Securities and Exchange Commission filed a civil suit accusing the former
OMB chief of "unsafe and unsound banking practices,"
"fraud," and "deceit" while he was a banker in Georgia.

Lance is dead. Long live the president.

II

The "Weirdo Factor"

James Earl Carter, Junior, is a Baptist. Harry Truman was too. John Kennedy was a Catholic. Gerald Ford, an Episcopalian; Richard Nixon, a Quaker. Congressman Morris Udall is a former Morman. George Wallace is a United Methodist; Senator Henry Jackson, an Episcopalian. Ronald Reagan is a member of the Christian Church and sometimes worships at Presbyterian services.

Presidents, former presidents, and also-rans all. Only Jimmy Carter openly claimed that he had "no doubt" but that "my campaign for the presidency is what God wants me to do."

Born in 1924, by 1935 Jimmy Carter had reached an age of "accountability." He was ushered to the Plains, Georgia, Baptist Church and there dunked, fully-clothed, in a large tub of water, baptized as a member of the spiritual flock of the heavenly shepherd. Some thirty years later, a defeated and demoralized Georgia gubernatorial candidate in his early forties, Jimmy Carter was "born again"; reborn into a more intimate union with Jesus Christ. And less than a decade later he was pursuing the American presidency, telling people that he was "running for president because I'm a deeply religious person."

Was Jimmy Carter—Sunday school teacher, hymn-singing, Bible-quoting, twice-born evangelical Christian—a preacher or a politician? Was he seeking a

57

council seat in the City of God or the City of Man? Some supporters liked his religion; others, his religiosity. Many critics were fearful of both: he was a hypocrite, a dissembler, a demagogue.

Washington *Post* political analyst Jules Witcover surmised that religion "plagued Carter throughout the long election year." Others claimed it carried him—miraculously—to the White House, "millions of Christians rallied to his banner." If religion was Jimmy Carter's cross, it was also his political salvation. His long-time strategist and confidant Hamilton Jordan unabashedly said it was simply "the weirdo factor."

Unlike the reception accorded John Kennedy's Catholicism in the 1960 presidential campaign—where fears focused primarily on whether the senator would wed the Romans to Washington—Jimmy Carter and his evangelical ways were oddities—unknown to the national press, the eastern establishment and a good many Americans living outside the South. He was the son of H. L. Mencken's Bible Belt. His life, he began admitting late in the campaign, "had been shaped in the church. I never knew anything except going to church." Even if one believed in his sincerity, the lingering doubt was whether a vote for Carter was a vote for a president or a priest. The Southern Baptists, the candidate's co-religionists, were considered the theological storehouse of the remnants of the Puritan tradition: a disciplined group of spiritualists with a reputation for claiming a flock that included non-smokers, teetotalers, evangelicals, red-necks and Klansmen; a religious sect that had always seemed to live on the outer banks of mainstream American culture.

Jimmy Carter and his religion seemed to break upon the American political arena more like the Reverend Sun Myung Moon and his flock of "moonies" descending upon Yankee Stadium. They were, as historian James T. Baker wrote, "virtual strangers . . ., oddities, objects of scorn. . . ."

Weird, indeed. "When a fellow starts telling how religious he is," said Senator Jackson, "I sort of become suspicious. I've taught Sunday school, but I'm not making my relationship with the Lord an issue in this campaign." Jackson, of course, faded into the obscurity of a dark political night while Jimmy Carter was telling voters that his favorite song was "Amazing Grace, how sweet the sound that saved a wretch like me. . ."

The 1976 campaign, by dint of candidate Carter's persistent proselytising, turned political truisms inside out. The "weirdo factor" became an agent for normalcy. Politics became religion. Jimmy Carter progressed from being unknown—a political liability in any election—to being an enigma—a blessing to the voters in 1976 who were already sated with the known. Rather than a plague, Carter's godliness came to be seen as a potential political panacea for the nation's spiritual malaise.

Even well-heeled political observers sensed that Carter was on to something as he chiseled out the religious niche for his own. One thing he had figured out, "Carter's secret," wrote journalist Richard Reeves in *New York* magazine, was "that what national leaders and other candidates perceive as a political crisis is actually a spiritual crisis."

Carter's religious campaign was waged on two fronts. First, and from the beginning, he appealed to a generalized feeling of spiritual discontent. Secondly, he promoted himself as a man who could be trusted because he was a "deeply religious person."

Jimmy Carter was, said Reeves, "one sharp country politician" who was just shrewd enough to use "the symbolism of Christianity" as an effective political weapon.

He everywhere blurred the distinction between sacred and secular. He appropriated the ethos and ethics of

Christianity and subtly welded them to his political campaign. In announcing his candidacy on December 12, 1974, he told the National Press Club that ". . . our trust has been betrayed. In our homes or at worship we are ever reminded of what we ought to do and what we ought to be. Our government can and must represent the best and highest ideals. . . ." He submerged political sentiments in a sentimental religious soup. In his autobiography *Why Not The Best?* —which he casually claimed was "a kind of summing up of my opinions about our nation"—Carter wrote:

> I have come to realize that in every person there is something fine and pure and noble, along with a desire for self-fulfillment. Political and religious leaders must attempt to provide a society within which these human attributes can be nurtured and enhanced. . . .
> I would hasten to point out that nowhere in the Constitution of the United States, or the Declaration of Independence, or the Bill of Rights, or the Emancipation Proclamation, or the Old Testament or the New Testament do you find the words 'economy' or 'efficiency.' Not that these two words are unimportant. But you discover other words like honesty, integrity, fairness, liberty, justice, courage, patriotism, compassion, love . . . words which describe what a government of human beings ought to be.

Bringing man to "self-fulfillment" was normally a task left to religion. Carter saw no paradox in asking that a government be both compassionate and just; the dictates of love and compassion would hardly send someone to the electric chair or allow even a President of the United States to earn more than two hundred thousand dollars a year while some child goes hungry living in a ghetto only a few blocks from the White House. Jimmy Carter thought it possible to be both preacher and politician; but in the end, as *Harper's* magazine editor Lewis Lapham observed, "he was elected to redeem the country, not to govern it." He was soon to find out that government was as incapable of redeeming a country as religion was of governing it.

Before Carter became enmeshed in the debilitating consequences of his spiritual politics, however, he began running amok with the questions about his personal religion, his Southern Baptist puritanism, his fundamental Biblical moralism, his "intimate" relationship with Jesus Christ, his absolute confidence that God's will was that he wage a campaign for the presidency—and what effect all this shirtsleeve piety would have on his ability to govern.

One remembered the last time religion had been an issue in a national election and how diligently John Kennedy backed away from it. In a 1960 speech to the Greater Houston Ministerial Association, Kennedy emphasized his belief "in a president whose views on religion are his own private affair."

By the time of the 1976 general election, however, the Democratic standard-bearer had not only become the candidate of love and compassion but also of religion. Religious commentators looked back on the campaign as if it had been a reenactment of the Biblical battle between David and Goliath. Books pouring out of religious publishing houses carried titles like *The Miracle of Jimmy Carter, The Church That Produced A President, A Southern Baptist in the White House, The Religion of President Carter.* According to one, Carter had become "one of the best things to happen to American evangelical Christianity in this century," the new crusader for an estimated fifty million evangelicals in the country.

Carter, it seemed, had rediscovered a new "silent majority." "There is a hidden religious power base in American culture," Catholic writer Michael Novak proclaimed, and "Jimmy Carter has found it." Fellow Baptist and history professor James Baker believed that "Carter had won by gaining the votes of people who claim Jesus."

The irony was that Carter only grudgingly took up the standard. He discovered the political blessings of publicizing his personal religion—his born-again, Baptist faith— only late in his four-year pursuit of national power; and only as a response, by Carter's admission, to increasing pressure from the press. It was Richard Reeves' "Carter's Secret" article for *New York* magazine in mid-March, 1976, that, according to Carter, precipitated the "surge of questioning" about his religion and in turn prompted him to come clean about his "intimate relationship" with Jesus. Until that time, he had spoken only perfunctorily about the separation of church and state and had stayed away from all but generalized allusions to his own religious experience. Only later would he remember that "my life has been shaped by the Church."

He made no mention of it in his now-famous autobiography *Why Not The Best?*, first published in October of 1975, almost a year after he formally announced his candidacy. The tome was touted as "the only book that reveals the real Jimmy Carter," but compared with what Carter was to "reveal" later in the campaign, it was more than skimpy on details illustrating a life that was supposedly molded by the church. He devoted a page and a half to the wonders of boiled peanuts—"one of the great gifts of God to mankind"—and credited them with an unforgettable moral lesson: "The good people, I thought, were the ones who bought boiled peanuts from me! I have spent much time since then in trying to develop my ability to judge other people, but that was the simplest method I ever knew, despite its limitations. I think about this every time I am tempted to judge other people hastily."

The boiled peanut episode—at the age of six—would seem to have played a much larger part in his character building than the local Baptist church, if lineage in his book is any criteria. In describing his early life, he mentions the church only twice, and then only to say that "we attended the Plains Baptist Church, where my father was a Sunday School teacher" or that "total membership . . . was about 300, but we ordinarily had and still have about 150 at Sunday School for each service. It is by far the biggest church in town." There was no reference to his baptism at age eleven, usually an important event in the life of devout believers. In painting the picaresque tableau of his early life, the future President seemed much more concerned with imparting an image of a freckle-faced, down-home, hard-working farm boy of the fields and swamps and streams and woods than of a life supposedly "shaped by the church." It was a curious omission in a book that promised "the real Jimmy Carter . . . in his own words."

But when "the media began to emphasize my beliefs," late in the primary season, just after the Reeves article and just before a Washington *Post* feature on his sister Ruth Stapleton, Carter decided "to tell the truth about it, not to conceal it but reveal it." It sounded like the admission of a spiritual cover-up.

In fact, Carter's evangelical, faith-healing sister acted as the unwitting catalyst in Jimmy's decision to confess. First, in early March 1976, Mrs. Stapleton, who had been diligently campaigning for her brother, decided to let some voters know about "a most important facet of Jimmy, one that couldn't possibly be pursued with any depth by the press or television." That "quality" was, she explained in a letter sent to a few hundred voters just prior to the March sixteenth Illinois primary, his "deep personal commitment to Jesus Christ and his will to serve Him in whatever capacity he finds himself." Many were already impressed by the politics of Jimmy Carter, she said, but "what usually is ignored in such analyses is that our nation's greatest need is for a President who will render spiritual leadership."

The country should be "under His blessings and guidance," said the candidate's sister, so "please pray for Jimmy." Jimmy had not yet been as explicit, but he hadn't objected to the letter.

Then, in the course of an interview with *Post* writer Myra McPherson prior to the mid-March North Carolina primary, Ruth recounted the story of a "deeply religious experience" Jimmy had after losing the 1966 Georgia gubernatorial race. Carter had already written that the defeat had been "extremely disappointing" and had gained some notoriety for his steely determined reference to the admonition "You show me a good loser and I will show you a loser. I did not intend to lose again." But, to her brother's chagrin, Ruth expanded on the depths of his disappointment. The two of them had taken a long walk through a pine forest after Jimmy's loss to Lester Maddox.

At one point Jimmy sat down, "put his face in his hands and cried like a baby."

"You and I are both Baptists," Ruth remembered him saying, "but what is it that you have that I haven't got?"

"What it amounts to in religious terms is total commitment," said Ruth. "I belong to Jesus. Everything I am."

Carter answered, "Ruth, that's what I want."

Brother and sister then discussed the burdens of such a commitment. Giving up money, friends and family would not be a problem, they agreed. "What about political ambitions?" she asked.

But he balked. He wanted to be governor. "I would use it for the people!"

Carter later told *Newsday*'s Washington bureau chief Martin Schram that "there was never any one time when I sat in my sister's presence weeping. That's been exaggerated grossly. . . . Ruth and I had a long talk and it was a very important conversation for me, but there was no flash of revelations, no weeping." But Ruth's story so surprised

Washington *Post* editors that they dispatched correspondent Jules Witcover to ask Carter for his reaction.
Witcover caught up with him just before a fund-raising
gathering at wealthy supporter's home in Winston-Salem
and told him of McPherson's article. It was "accurate, ba-
sically," said Carter, but he didn't "cry like a baby."

At the fund-raiser, a question from the audience gave
the candidate a chance to take the offensive, beat the press
to the story. He bared his religious soul before some
seventy-five well-to-do political backers. It was in 1967, he
announced, that he had a "deeply profound religious experience that changed my life dramatically." He wouldn't
go into details, he said, but it was then that "I recognized
for the first time that I had lacked something very
precious—a complete commitment to Christ, a presence
of the Holy Spirit in my life in a more profound and personal way. . . . And I formed a very close, intimate, personal relationship with God, through Christ, that has given
me a great deal of peace."

And Jimmy Carter was off and running on yet another
religious track, claiming to have some sort of hotline to the
Almighty. Politically, it may have been a wise decision.
North Carolina was a heavily Baptist state. Jimmy Carter
knew it; and many political observers thought it contrib-
uted to his victory. "The people in North Carolina knew
what I was talking about," said Carter. He wouldn't have
done it in Boston: people there wouldn't have understood.
He attempted to allay suspicions that he may not have
been so honest were it not for the prodding of the press.
"In retrospect," he claimed, "I would have done the same
thing. I don't see any legitimate alternative to it. The
people have a right to understand the religious beliefs of
their future President."

But Carter's revelations only further clarified the inex-
tricable mix that the candidate saw in religion and politics.

He looked more like a preacher than politician. When he had first decided to enter politics and run for the Geogia Senate in 1962, Carter had asked a minister for his opinion. "If you want to be of service to other people," the pastor told him, "why don't you go into the ministry or into some honorable social service work?" The immediate response was, "How would you like to be the pastor of a church with eighty thousand members?" (a reference to the residents of the fourteenth senate district).

Though he would deny ever looking on the presidency as a pastorate for two hundred fifteen million souls— despite his sister's suggestion that he would be "a President who will render spiritual leadership"—his "complete commitment to Christ" and his overt declarations of confidence in knowing the will of God, left one wondering whether Jimmy Carter could look at the American nation as anything but a pastorate. He was muddled either in self-deception or hypocrisy.

It was impossible to know what the candidate meant when he steadfastly maintained that he believed in "absolute and total separation of church and state," while, in campaigning for the office of chief representative of the state, he continually stressed his intimate and unequivocably loyal relationship with the church's supreme commander. Even his favorite theologian, Reinhold Niebuhr, whom Carter was fond of quoting, had warned that "religion is more frequently a source of confusion than of light in the political realm. The tendency to equate our political with our Christian convictions causes politics to generate idolatry." But weaving in and out of the campaign and tagging along into the presidency was Jimmy Carter's inability and unwillingness to distinguish between the two. He told the Southern Baptist Convention in 1974 that in every aspect of life—home, office, church, and government—"we should continually strive for perfection

as commanded by God." "God's laws," he told a Bible class
in his new church in the nation's capital in early 1977, "are
the same in Washington, D.C., and in Plains, Georgia, and
in Russia, China, and Pakistan. ... Congress meets and
Congress goes home. But God's laws do not change."
Jimmy Carter, claiming a direct line to the inspiration of
the immutable Solon, was seeking a job as a powerful law-
maker in the temporal world, a complicated world, a world
with devilish Russians, obstreperous politicians and per-
plexing problems of faltering economies, nuclear arms
proliferation, dilapidated cities, welfare, unemployment,
inefficient government, oppressive government, polluted
rivers, too few energy supplies and too many taxes. "It is a
sentimental illusion," commented former Princeton chap-
lain and author of *The Nixon Theology* Charles Henderson,
"to believe that complex political problems can be solved
by an appeal to 'compassion and love.'"

Former presidential adviser and historian Arthur
Schlesinger, Jr., sounded the same complaint. He saw Carter's campaign overloaded with the disconcerting "implication that evangelical principles can solve social, economic
and international perplexities." He called Niebuhr in to
support him. "American Christianity," wrote the theologian, "tends to be irrelevant to the problems of justice
because it persists in presenting the law of love as a simple
solution for every communal problem." Carter's constantly recurring promise that he would restore "a government that is as good and honest and decent and compassionate and as filled with love as are the American
people," was wistful sermonizing. And Niebuhr, said
Schlesinger, "would have dismissed this belief in the inherent virtue of people en masse as the most arrant sentimen-
talism."

In any case, Carter hardly evinced much confidence in
his belief in the goodness, honesty, decency, compassion

and love of the American people and his desire to fashion a government equally so, when he took positions on issues such as favoring the death penalty on the one hand and disapproving of abortion on the other.

Much of Jimmy Carter's impressionistic approach to politics—some preferred to call it duplicity; others, like author and biographer of both George Wallace and Billy Graham, Marshall Frady, believed that "Carter utterly subscribed to all of his platitudes and homilies"—was rooted in his Southern Baptist origins.

The denomination, Protestantism's largest, was an odd mixture—fundamentalism, an intense evangelical missionary spirit, puritanism, revivals, personal salvation divorced from good works, rebirth, and no dogma—and represented something of an enigma and curiosity not only for secular America, but also for those nurtured in more doctrinaire and hierarchical religious institutions.

Their theology was something of an anti-theology, a religion without a creed, founded on a belief in a very personal and intimate communion with Jesus Christ. For them (and, they believe, for everyone else) salvation came only as a gift of God. Some have it, some don't. It could not be earned; it was there for the taking, offered to anyone who heard the Word and accepted it. The Bible, literally interpreted, was thus the bedrock of faith and action. The New Testament must speak for itself—without the complicated mediating of academic theologians or priests. If one wanted to know what the Baptists believed, "he can read the New Testament," said Carter. Jesus had prescribed a spiritual cleansing by total immersion and it was thus that eleven-year-old Jimmy Carter was baptized. Christ told the wealthy Jew Nicodemus that to "be saved" he had to be "born again" and so Jimmy Carter experienced a second birth. Unlike other descendants of the reformation who continue to believe that salvation is a continuing process throughout life, the fiery preachers of the American South, like religious midwives, were anxious to see this rebirth burst upon an individual as an emotion-charged event, at a given moment in time. The fire and brimstone "revivals"—important annual events in the life of southern evangelicals—were not so much teaching sessions as they were plaintive calls for sinners to come home to God.

It was confusing to find the Southern Baptists insisting on the importance of the "priesthood of the believer" to emphasize their freedom from complex theologies and overbearing creeds while the Southern Baptist Convention issued frequent condemnations of alcohol, gambling, extramarital sex, smoking and—sometimes—dancing. Despite its claim that the thirty-five thousand churches in the convention were autonomous and democratic, the convention perceived its role as "the mightiest force for world evangelism on the contemporary scene."

Southern Baptists, like their preeminent political representative, successful businessman Jimmy Carter, also seemed to have little difficulty in accepting the sanctity of the secular word, a prediliction which helped make them a powerful force—if not the "mightiest"—in the economic world as well.

Carter's Southern Baptist church owned property valued at some five billion dollars and counted among its more worldly members R. J. Reynolds (tobacco), W. Maxey Jarman (Genesco's executive committee chairman, trustee of the Moody Bible Institute and author of *A Businessman Looks At The Bible*), and Owen Cooper (past president of the Southern Baptist Convention and a director of the Federal Reserve Board in Atlanta).

The pension fund for the ministers of the convention controlled more than three million shares in one hundred sixty-four different companies, including prominent corporations headquartered in the south like Coca-Cola, Burlington Industries, Genuine Parts, Knight-Ridder, and Southern Railway. "There should be no investments in, nor loans to," stated the fund's portfolio guidelines, "companies known to be non-cooperative with fair employment practices, improvement of pollution problems, and generally recognized social, health, and other national issues." But, as journalist Alexander Cockburn reported, the Baptist holdings included stock in Amax, "one of the biggest strip-mine operators in the world," J. P. Stevens Textile Co., "known as the worst labor-law violator in the nation," and Union Carbide, "the first U.S. company to break the UN embargo on Rhodesian chrome."

Jimmy Carter, known for his diligence and shrewdness as a peanut entrepreneur once boasted "I've got a good business and I've got a lot of employees and I make good money." In 1976 Carter owned with his mother and brother one thousand one hundred acres of farmland, two thousand acres of swamp and timberland, a warehousing business and equipment worth some five million dollars. It had never been easy to distinguish the just boundaries of the City of God and the City of Man; but Jimmy Carter and the Southern Baptists seemed willing to promote the interests of both as if God's portfolio would include a Coca-Cola company. (And it just might, if one could believe the Coke commercials: "I'd like to build the world a home and furnish it with love, grow apple trees, and honey bees, and snow-white turtle doves.")

The Southern Baptists often defended themselves poorly. The president of Southern Baptist Seminary, Duke K. McCall, attacked journalists who had "ventilated a lot of half-baked tripe in their columns and on the air." Even national television news commentators, he continued, were "plain incompetent, not because they did not

know about Southern Baptists before Jimmy Carter broke
on the scene, but because they did not bother to do
adequate research." So McCall attempted to clear the waters: "Southern Baptists really are different. We cannot
make ourselves look like the main line church bodies in
America. On the spectrum of religious bodies in the
United States we are right-wing, evangelical. . . . Paint us
purple with passion if a public official advocates any form
of gambling. Color us absent in the ecumenical meetings.
Paint us red with rage if one of our leaders takes a stand on
a public issue with which individually we do not agree. . . ."

It was not the kind of statement which placated the
doubting Thomases. Talking to *Newsweek* magazine just before the general election, Albert Outler of Southern
Methodist University harangued the Southern Baptists,
voicing a complaint that by then had become common.
"The fact is," said Outler, adding a critical twist to McCall's
description, "that Southern Baptist's have been culturally
isolated and are theologically unsophisticated." Their
adamant insistence on political leaders who know what the
Word of God is, is no less than a hankering after "theoc-
racy, and their Napoleon, whether he likes it or not, is
Jimmy Carter." (Jimmy Carter professed not to like it. "I
have never felt that the Lord required me to run for president, or that I'm ordained to be president.")

If Outler was accusing the Southern Baptists of being a
group of theological Neanderthals, there was worry that
Carter too was theologically unsophiticated. Syndicated
columnist Garry Wills once asked the candidate—"a man
who reads the Bible every day, and has taught it all his
adult life"—whether he ever used Rudolph Bultmann's
"form criticism" in his analysis of the Biblical text. "What is
that?" asked Carter. A "dumbfounded" Wills had to explain; and concluded that "for a bright and educated

modern man, dealing with the thing he says matters most to him, he shows an extraordinarily reined-in curiosity. It suggests a kind of willed narrowness of mastery."

Carter did find it "hard to question Holy Scripture." To understand his beliefs, those of the Baptists, simply "read the New Testament," he suggested. Theologically, his hands were tied, his eyes narrowly focused backward two thousand years. ". . . I can't change the teachings of Christ," he protested. "I can't change the teachings of Christ! I believe in them. . . ."

He claimed to have flirted with modern, unorthodox (from the traditional Baptists' point of view) theologians like Niebuhr and Paul Tillich, but it must have been a very selective dalliance. In fact, Tillich—"one of my favorite philosophers or theologians"—would probably have been as dumbfounded as Wills to find that Carter was, at heart, a fundamentalist who could not see the Bible either as a historical document or a part of a broader spiritual tradition. "The Bible as such," wrote Tillich, is not "the norm of Christian theology but the Bible insofar as it is the genuine witness to the new reality. . . . It is a rather naive illusion of some Protestants to believe that by jumping over two thousand years of Christian tradition they can come into a direct and existential . . . relation to the biblical texts."

But as with his proclaimed intimate relation with Christ, Carter seemed to be wedded to the literal words of the Bible—with no intermediaries. He did admit once that he had "trouble with Paul sometimes, especially when he says that a woman's place is with her husband, and that she should keep quiet and cover her head in church. I just can't go along with him on that." But he offered no clue to the criteria he used for selecting what he chose to believe in, and left one wondering whether God's laws were absolute only when Jimmy Carter declared them so.

Paul's biblical advice could be dismissed. But, as Carter told a late-evening campaign audience in the early primaries, "The Bible says that adultery and fornication are wrong. I believe in the Bible. I believe that premarital and extramarital sex are wrong." Sometimes the Bible was Carter's moral bedrock, other times, not. If there was a logic or consistency in his approach to the Scripture and morality it was hidden away within Carter himself.

Carter continually wrapped himself in a blanket of moral rectitude. He preached to New Hampshire high school students in early 1976 that "obviously the moral thing to do is to abstain from intercourse unless you are married." Carter's desire to appeal to the spiritual void that he sensed existed in the nation—"our trust has been betrayed"—seemed to push him to the extreme of preachments on personal morality. "Every time I hear a politician talk about morality," said theologian Michael Novak, "my stomach tells me he is out to get me, even if at first I can't see how . . . American coins have it correct: 'In God We Trust.' Meaning, no one else. Not in political leaders. Not even in government. 'Our people are losing faith in America,' Nixon said. But America is not a religion." Inevitably Carter became trapped by what New York *Times* campaign reporter James Wooten called "his supermorality."

Such was the image he painted of himself that when Carter, in the course of an interview with Norman Mailer for the New York *Times Magazine*, said "I don't care if people say—," and he actually said the famous four-letter word that the *Times* has not printed in the one-hundred-twenty-five years of its publishing life—the non-religionist novelist was moved to remark that Carter "got it out without a backing-up of phlegm or a hitch in his rhythm . . ., as if he, too, had to present his credentials to that part of the twentieth century personified by his interviewer."

He continued to drive the moral high road in his interview with *Playboy* magazine. "Committing adultery," he said confidently, "according to the Bible—which I believe in—is a sin. For us to hate one another, for us to have sexual intercourse outside marriage, for us to engage in homosexual activities, for us to steal, for us to lie—all these are sins." *Playboy* pushed on about morality, finally asking about the "self-righteousness" and "moral certainty" of the candidate's remarks. Has Carter himself "ever been wrong, has he ever had a failure of nerve?" "Well," Carter began, "there are a lot of things I could have done differently had I known during my early life what I now know." He then carefully ticked off a list of subjunctives— ". . . *would certainly have spoken* out more clearly and loudly on the civil rights issue. . . . *would have demanded* that our nation never get involved initially in the Vietnam War . . . *would have told* the country in 1972 that Watergate was . . . a horrible crime"—without admitting that his support of either the war or Richard Nixon may, in fact, have actually been mistakes, even "in hindsight." (As *Harper's* editor Lapham suggested later, when remarking on Carter's presidency, "Having already been absolved of sin, Mr. Carter obviously can do no wrong.")

A little farther on in the interview, however, in response to the famous, final question, the Baptist candidate was admitting to lusting after women, saying "shack-up" and "screw," and on his way to shocking an electorate that had come to believe in his supermorality. In the aftermath of the interview a Harris poll gave the Southerner only a slim seven percentage point lead over Gerald Ford, almost a twenty point slide since the festive post-nomination days.

Carter ended his *Playboy* monologue on religion, morality, sin, lust and sex wtih the remark "I don't inject these beliefs in my answers to your secular questions," as if to emphasize his desire not to impose his personal moral standards on others. He then "clenched his fist and gestured sharply," called Richard Nixon and Lyndon Johnson liars (the latter to his embarrassing regret when he arrived in Texas to find the longhorn state's democrats still loyal to their native son) and insisted that his "religious beliefs alone would prevent that from happening to me." It was Carter's perennial secret, his mystery, his paradox that he could claim in one breath with utter sincerity his intention to keep religion out of politics and the affairs of others and in the next promise not to repeat the mistakes of past presidents because of "religious beliefs alone."

Yes, he affirmed, he believed in "absolute and total separation of church and state." But yes, too, he was committed to Christ and was "running for president because I'm a deeply religious person." And no, he didn't "look on [the presidency] with religious connotations." "If Mr. Carter were not in such dead earnest," wrote professor Schlesinger, "about both his theology and his political philosophy, his failure to reconcile them, or even to admit that they are at odds, would almost lead to the conclusion that he was engaged in cynical flattery of the people. . . ."

Jimmy Carter seemed incapable of seeing the necessary distinctions between a political and a religious world; of recognizing the fact that government was not established to bring men to God, or could somehow represent a goodness and decency and honesty and compassion and love that my have filled the American people as a religious ideal but certainly didn't as either historical fact or political possibility. "Why has government been instituted at all?" asked founding father Alexander Hamilton. "Because the passions of men will not conform to the dictates of reason and justice, without constraint."

Carter carried his religion on to the central stage of the political theater. "His identity is so bound up with his religion," said the president's new Baptist pastor in Washington, "that it would do considerable damage to him as a person to be separated from that." And only three weeks after the inauguration he was once again preaching to a secular audience. He was no longer candidate Carter, however, wooing votes or assuaging doubts abut what he may or may not do; his words now carried the weight of power inherent in the office of the presidency. In a question and answer session with employees of the Department of Housing and Urban Development in early February the president outlined some of his plans for the future: he would extend the White House intern program throughout the government; he didn't intend to establish a cabinet post for equal employment opportunity, but did want more progress in the hiring of women and other minorities; he didn't know what he would do about establishing "flexi-time" for government workers. Then, something "that just came to mind." "We can't forget," said the president (now speaking for "all of us in Government"), "that we need a stable family life to make us better servants of the people. So those of you who are living in sin, I hope you'll get married." There was scattered laughter, but Carter continued, "I think it's very important that we have stable family lives. And I am serious about that."

Later that year, when asked at a press conference whether he "held anything against people in your organization who were involved promiscuously with other women," Carter said no, that he couldn't hold it against people "who had a different standard from myself." But then, as if remembering that "promiscuity" could be as much a political sin as a religious one—the Wilbur Mills/Fanny Fox and Wayne Hays/Elizabeth Ray episodes the most recent examples of political flights from grace—he added, "I've done everything I could—well, properly and legitimately—to encourage my staff members' families to be stable and I have also encouraged the same sort of thing in my Cabinet." What *action* would the president take if there were sexual indiscretions among his employees? "If there are some who slip from grace," he concluded, "then I can only say that I'll do the best I can to forgive them and pray for them."

Carter seemed compelled to sermonize, but a pastor in the White House seemed to mean that religious beliefs tended to become a sort of religious policy. Those personal beliefs not only trickled into the smallest of decisions—terminating the practice of serving hard liquor at White House dinners—but also acted as a springboard and justification for sticky domestic and foreign policy actions. In Jimmy Carter's transition from candidate to president, the Word was made flesh; but the flesh appeared weak.

What was a boon in the campaign often proved a boondoggle in the presidency. Trust and love suddenly seemed conspicuously insufficient to the tasks of government. Perhaps more was needed than "to forgive them and pray for them." It was surely not enough when Bert Lance, the president's first appointee, came under fire. Nevertheless, Carter was on his knees on September 21, 1977, praying with his Director of the Budget hours before the former Georgia banker resigned his post in a storm of controversy and suspicion over his financial wheelings-and-dealings back in the Peach state. In August, the president had said he knew "nothing of anything illegal or even unethical that Bert Lance has ever done." He was still clinging to that position on the day he announced Lance's departure, appealing as he did during the campaign to the nation's willingness to take him at his word and trust in his sincerity. "I know him personally as well as if he was my own brother," he said at the nationally televised news conference. "He's close to me," said Carter. And echoing the religious sentiment he repeated so often as a candidate, Carter claimed that he had "always trusted Bert Lance to do the proper and the unselfish thing. His honesty and integrity have been proven." The president's sentiments seemed to have little to do with the political realities, however, as Lance's problems nagged Carter into the following year—and for his part, still trusting, the president bestowed on his deposed budget director a VIP diplomatic passport for his foreign travels—until April of 1978 when his friend and "brother" was accused in a civil complaint filed by the Securities and Exchange Commission and the Comptroller of the Currency of "unsafe and unsound banking practices," "deceit," and "fraud." The prayers and trust and brotherhood and honor and closeness seemed to have numbed Carter's political sensibilities when he needed them most, and did nothing to spur confidence in either the politician who said "our government in Washington ought to be an inspiration to us all," or the Baptist Sunday school teacher who told his class that Jesus is a teacher "of the way you're supposed to act, a very gentle way, a clear way, based on simplicity and truth."

Even in more narrowly defined religious matters President Carter was able to deny political realities by wrapping them in an amorphous religiousity. A few months before the Lance resignation,he walked into a sticky hometown racial quarrel which had split his Baptist brethren into two feuding factions. The Plains Baptist Church first became the focus of a civil rights controversy after a black minister had tried—and failed—to gain admittance just two days before the general election. Doubts about Carter's "real" attitudes toward blacks ran rampant at the time, especially when it was learned that the church—where the candidate had been baptized forty years before and to which he belonged most of his adult life—had banned blacks from its services in 1965. An eleventh-hour compromise repeal of the ban, for which Carter was given credit, was passed, but it didn't stick. And the continuing feud over black admissions eventually resulted in the forced departure of integrationist pastor Bruce Edwards and the formation of a splinter church.

When Carter decided to travel to Plains in August of 1977, he knew he was stuck between a rock and a hard place. Not only were many of his friends now members of either the Plains Baptist or the breakaway Maranatha church but his presence at either one would signify an endorsement of its position.

As Chief of State in the week prior to the Plains church services, Carter was busy fulfilling his promise to be an "activist" president—if not one anxious to shorten the arm of the federal government: signing into law the bill to establish a new Energy Department with a projected budget of $10.6 billion and a staff that would number twenty thousand; announcing proposals for solving the illegal alien problem that included an increase of two-thousand new Border Patrol agents on the Mexican-American boundary; and, in a last-minute decision, shelving his goal of keeping a lid on welfare spending by unveiling a "Program for Better Jobs and Income" that would add almost three-billion-dollars to the total cost of existing welfare programs. He was on his way to confronting one of the political realities he didn't have to face as a candidate— that he could not be all things to all people.

And in Plains on that summer Sunday of August seventh, Carter solved the problem of which warring church to attend—a decision he "faced with considerable trepidation" according to *Times* reporter James Wooten—with an artful gesture of political transparency: he went to both, a gesture which seemed to be an endorsement of the split itself. At Maranatha, Carter was asked to give the benediction and he prayed that "there be a permanence about this church based on love and forgiveness and dedication."

"O Father," he said, "bless this small and new church, separated, we all pray, not out of a sense of estrangement or alienation or division or hatred, but out of a sense of rededication to thee.*

Despite the fact the schism had resulted from struggles over racial integration, Carter, who had claimed as a personal "fault" his inability "to compromise on any principle I believe is right," preferred not only to skirt the question but, in effect, to lend credence to the narrow-mindedness which precipitated it. "It's a healthy thing to have two strong churches," he said afterwards. "They're both good churches . . ." Though preaching love and reconciliation, Carter sounded more the clanging cymbal, hollow and out of tune."

Even his fellow Southern Baptists spoke more forcefully. Gathering in Kansas City for their annual meeting, the convention on June sixteenth had adopted a resolution that affirmed "our belief in the free exercise of religion as determined by a free conscience" and opposed "any discrimination, legal or otherwise, against any individual based upon race, age, gender, or nationality."

In the end, both the Plains church feud and the Bert Lance affair were examples not so much of Carter's insincerity to ideals as of his inability to choose between conflicting ideals. And the result in both instances was misguided, ineffective and—in the Lance case, at least—ethically questionable actions.

The chinks in the Carter armor that had been visible, though largely ignored in a general suspension of disbelief, during the campaign grew larger in the presidency. His confusion about the distinctions between politics and religion and his moral rectitude had led him to moral

---

*The President's prayers were, in fact, answered. A year after his visit, Maranatha's congregation had more than doubled in size—to sixty-eight members—was planning a building program and continuing to stick by its unconditional "open-door" policy. "This is permanent," said pastor Fred Collins. "We won't be getting back together in one church."

preachments on adultery and fornication from his "bully pulpit" and shattered his crystalline ethical standards as he stubbornly refused to admit that trusting Bert Lance had nothing to do with past banking practices. The president's high-mindedness and moral idealism, rather than adding balance and vision to pragmatic action, was complicating and contradicting his daily politics.

When he looked beyond the borders of the United States, the same religious and moral fervor seemed to fire his world view while stifling a global strategy. Immediately upon assuming office, he curiously shouldered the role of world leader in a campaign for human rights, bringing to an end what New York *Times* columnist Anthony Lewis called the "years of silence in the face of tyranny and brutality." What was curious, however, was that, as Senator Daniel Moynihan pointed out, "Human rights as an issue in foreign policy was by no means central to Jimmy Carter's campaign for the presidency." He backed into human rights in much the same way that he slid subtly into advertising his personal religion.

In his announcement speech at the end of 1974, Carter mentioned human rights only once and then only to suggest that "this country set a standard within the community of nations." It was a cheerworthy ideal, but not a new one. And he was no more specific in his one reference to human rights at the Democractic convention when, in ticking off a neo-Gandhian list of definitions of peace in his acceptance speech—"not the mere absence of war . . . action to stamp out international terrorism . . . demonstration of strength and good will"—he said that "Peace is the unceasing effort to preserve human rights." In fact, in the Democratic platform drafting committee and at the convention, the Carter people seemed to have little to say about the question. "The Carter representatives," said Moynihan, a member of the platform committee, "were at best neutral, giving the impression of not having heard very much of the matter before and not having any particular views."

After the convention, however, Carter, if still lacking a *particular* policy on human rights, was anything but neglectful of preaching an absolute moral principle on the subject. In a September 1976 speech to one-thousand-five-hundred members of B'nai B'rith, a national Jewish organization, the candidate accused the Ford administration of putting "self-interest above principle" with the result that there was "little room for morality" in the conduct of foreign affairs. "We cannot look away," Carter vowed, "when a government tortures people, or jails them for their beliefs or denies minorities fair treatment or the right to emigrate." If other countries wanted United States support and friendship, said Carter, "they must understand that we want to see basic human rights respected by all governments."

This vision of global righteousness became so crucial by the time of the inauguration that when Carter's chief issues analyst, Stuart Eizenstat, completed his one-hundred-twenty-page interregnum summary of the hundreds of promises his boss had made during the campaign, the first major subject listed under "Foreign Policy" was "Moral Authority"; and the very first foreign policy promise was "never supporting nations which stand for principles with which their people violently disagree, and which are completely antithetical to our principles." In the course of a few short months, the Carter camp had come from having no "particular views" on the place of human rights in the formation of foreign policy to a principle which seemed to link all of America's international ties to human rights. "And the commitment," he told the nation on inaugural day, "must be absolute."

It was an apparently unvarying, objective, just and "absolute" moral concern. It was also one that began to dissolve in contradiction as soon as the new president moved from elocution to action.

From the start, Carter undermined his credibility. He may, for example, have inspired more confidence in his belief in the moral principle had he not resurrected old war heroes to implement it. Though he had often spoke of the "tragedy" and "quagmire" of Vietnam as if it were an archetypical example of an amoral policy conceived and executed in a moral vacuum, Carter chose Cyrus Vance for his Secretary of State, a man who had been general counsel to the Defense Department from 1961 to 1962, Secretary of the Army from 1962 to 1963, and Deputy Secretary of Defense from 1964 to 1967. Carter's new Defense Secretary, Harold Brown, had run the Air Force under Robert McNamara and once reportedly suggested the bombing of the civilian population of North Vietnam. And to fill the key position of Assistant to the President for National Security, Carter tabbed Zbigniew Brzezinski, who had served on the policy-planning staff of the State Department from 1966 to 1968 and had been one of the more outspoken of Vietnam war hawks. These men helped orchestrate the "tragedy," an integral part of the war establishment that candidate Carter said had "tremendously misled" the American people "about the immediate prospects for victory, about the level of our involvement, about the relative cost in American lives." President Carter, however, seemed to prefer not to punish the mistakes of the past as much as extoll the transgressors to repent and be saved. It was as if "the sin of Vietnam," as former State Department official Richard J. Barnet wrote in explaining Carter's human rights rationale, "would be expunged by working for redemption in the rest of the world." However noble the redemptive urge, Carter had immediately contradicted it.

But Carter was given the opportunity to take up the human rights banner during the first week of his administration and he seemed to grasp it like a modern-day Jean d'Arc. In a letter dated one day after the innauguration, Russia's most famous dissident, Nobel prize winner Andrei Sakharov, appealed to the new president "to defend those who suffer because of their nonviolent struggle for openness, for justice, for destroyed rights of other people." And it was Carter's "duty" he said "to fight for them." Against the advice of the State Department, which had forwarded Sakharov's letter to him with the suggestion that he not involve himself personally, Carter wrote to the Russian offering his assurance that "human rights is a central concern of my administration." And he went on to promise a continuation of his "firm commitment to promote respect for human rights not only in our own country but also abroad. We shall use our good offices to seek the release of prisoners of conscience, and we will continue our efforts to shape a world responsive to human aspirations . . ."

The Soviet reaction to the unusual presidential letter was immediate and not unexpected. The American president was interfering in their internal affairs, an action which would no doubt complicate negotiations on arms limitations. But rather than signal any retreat from the position taken in his letter, Carter reassured the Russians that he was not singling them out for criticism, that his principle would be universally applied, and had nothing to do with political ideologies. He wasn't attempting "to launch a unilateral criticism" of them, but was "trying to set a standard in our own country and make my concerns expressed throughout the world . . ." Unfortunately, however, Carter's subsequent actions betrayed his oratory.

A week after his assurances to Russia that they were not

being held up as an example, Carter was entertaining Soviet dissident emigré Vladimir Bukovsky in the Roosevelt Room of the White House. "Our commitment to the concept of human rights is permanent," he told the thirty-four-year-old Russian who had been freed from a Soviet prison camp only the previous December, "and I don't intend to be timid in my public statements and positions." Already Carter was trying to play on both sides of the street. His declaration of courage in "my public statements" was probably an attempt to cover over what was proving to be the timidity of his actions. Five days before the Bukovsky meeting, Secretary of State Vance had appeared before a Senate committee to ask, on behalf of the administration, for a reduction of foreign aid to Argentina, Uruguay, and Ethiopia because of human rights violations in those countries; but urged continued support of countries such as South Korea whose "repressive government" in the words of candidate Carter was "taking away liberty from their people," and "openly violates human rights . . . . We should use our tremendous influence to increase freedom." Not only had Carter reneged on a campaign promise, he had thrown his presidential promise of an unvarying application of human rights standards out the window. Supporting South Korea while admitting that there were serious violations of human rights was no way to convince the Russians that America was committed to a moral principle and not self-interested politics. Three weeks later, Carter was back on the moral high-road, promising the United Nations General Assembly on March seventeenth that America would be "steadfast in our dedication to the dignity and well-being of people throughout the world."

It seemed as if Carter was still waging a campaign against a government that he was somehow not associated with. The president would not be "timid" and he would affirm America's "permanent" commitment to freedom "throughout the world"; while his Secretary of State compromised and backtracked.

Significantly, Vance's first public speech as Secretary, at Law Day ceremonies at the University of Georgia Law School on April thirtieth, was titled "Human Rights and Foreign Policy." As if reacting to the inconsistent and confusing direction already apparent in the Carter administration's foreign policy (or lack thereof), Vance began by saying, "Our human rights policy must be understood in order to be effective." He then proceded to outline the strategy for a tactical retreat from the president's ideals, conceding that "we must always keep in mind the limits of our power and wisdom." He expressed concern about the dangers of attempting to "impose our values on others."*

"We must be realistic," he cautioned. "Our country can only achieve our objectives if we shape what we do to the case at hand." He then listed seventeen questions to be addressed when considering "the case at hand," suggesting, in effect, that pragmatism, not principle, would prevail. A day later, Carter was back proclaiming his "undeviating commitment" to human rights.

Only three months into the new reign and already two major contradictions shadowed the Carter human rights/ foreign affairs policy: first, the president had begun a retreat from his unswerving moral principles and cam-

---

*It seemed that Moscow had some hand in dampening the new administration's zeal. On March twenty-first, Soviet boss Leonid Brezhnev had issued a stern reproach to the Americans: "Washington's claims to teach others how to live cannot be accepted by any sovereign state . . . I will repeat again: We will not tolerate interference in our internal affairs by anyone and under any pretext." That rebuke was followed just a week and a half later by the collapse of arms limitations talks between Vance and Brezhnev in Moscow. It was not surprising, then, that Vance began to talk about "our values" when he mentioned human rights.

paign promises while he continued to blow the same rhetorical horn; second, the human rights actions that *were* taken in the context of foreign affairs exemplified not only a double standard, but an old, already used and abused one.

Both these problems were evident in Carter's commencement address at Notre Dame University on May twenty-second, the first major statement of foreign policy of his administration. Though again reaffirming "America's commitment to human rights as a fundamental tenet of our foreign policy," he hastened to point out that such a policy could not be conducted by "rigid moral maxims."

It was already obvious, however, that a "rigid" morality, not even a flexible one, had been applied to Indonesia, South Korea and the Philippines when the Carter administration refused to cut aid to them. None of those countries, according to conclusions in a report released by the State Department in February of 1978, would have qualified for aid had Carter stuck by his promise not to support "nations which stand for principles with which their people violently disagree, and which are completely antithetical to our principles." Said the State Department:

Republic of Korea Although excesses cannot be ruled out in isolated cases . . . we do not believe that torture is now regularly employed in South Korea . . . The Korean Government uses "Emergency Measures" authority to effect arrest, detention, search or seizure without warrant. Those measures conflict with international standards with respect to civil and political liberties . . . As of December 1977 we estimate that fewer than one-hundred-fifty persons remained in prison under Korean emergency measures . . . Police and security officials may enter and search the homes of suspects without warrant . . . There are sporadic reports of this authority being used in connection with cases of political dissenters . . . At the heart of the human rights problems in Korea is the restriction

of political liberties ... Emergency Measure No. 9 ... pro-
hibits specified political activities, including calls for constitutional revision and criticism of the emergency measure itself,
any political activities by students, and the reporting of activities prohibited under the emergency measure as well as the
spreading of "false rumors." ... more than five-hundred individuals have been charged at one time or another for violation of the currently enforced EM-9.

Indonesia The principal human rights problem in Indonesia
continues to be the detention without trial of large numbers
of persons believed by the government to have been associated with the 1965 Communist effort to seize power ... At
least three hundred thousand persons were detained under
the 1966 Emergency Powers Act on suspicion of complicity in
the attempted coup ... Approximately twenty-thousand are
reported by the Government of Indonesia to remain in detention without ... formal charges against them ... Statutes
which permit long detention without trial and which restrict
freedom of speech, of the press, and of movement within the
country are deeply ingrained in Indonesian history and tradition, although contrary to internationally recognized human
rights.

The Philippines ... governed by President Ferdinand Marcos
under martial law since 1972 ... Several organizations—
including Amnesty International, the Association of Major
Religious Superiors in the Philippines, and the International
Commission of Jurists—have investigated the Philippine situation and reported evidence of torture ... includ(ing) such
methods as water treatment, electric shock, long isolation and
physical beatings, leading in at least one case to death ... The
House Subcommittee on International Organizations reported in July 1977 its conclusion after "extensive testimony"
that some political prisoners have been subject to "cruel, in-
humane, and degrading treatment." ... There have been
many instances of prisoners being detained without charge or
trial, in some cases for more than five years ... Freedom of
expression ... is controlled by a variety of means ... The
mass communications media have been purged of critical or
independent voices.

Carter may have been committed to human rights in principle, but showed little desire to commit his administration to the application of any principle besides an inconsistent pragmatism.

In fact, "if it had the choice," commented New York *Times* Washington correspondent, Richard D. Burt, with considerable understatement, "the Carter administration would probably not have bothered to release the State Department's survey." There was, however, little choice in the matter. Before Carter had even assumed office, Congress had ordered the Department to report each year on the status of human rights in every country receiving United States aid.

Even Vance's dramatic announcement of aid cuts to Argentina, Uruguay, and Ethiopia because of their human rights violations was nothing more than a fulfillment, not of any Carter principle or commitment, but of previous Congressional mandates. Senator Henry Jackson, for example, had pushed through an amendment to the 1974 Trade Act which would deny favored nation status to countries that didn't allow its citizens reasonable emigration rights. In 1976 Congress cut off military aid completely to Chile and Uruguay on human rights grounds. And before Vance arrived on Capitol Hill in February, Congress had already indicated that it would do the same to Argentina and Ethiopia. According to the Washington *Post,* some congressmen were a bit miffed, calling the Carter administration's aid reduction proposals "cheap shots."

And while on the one hand the Carter administration seemed to be breaking no new ground on human rights policy—only its own promises and principles—on the other, it proved itself remarkably adept at changing even its own modest ground rules. (At least to the extent that the case-by-case approach outlined by Vance could be considered a rule.) Nicaragua was the most astonishing example of its confusion.

In April of 1977 the State Department testified at Congressional hearings that Nicaragua—the tiny Central American country where, in the words of *Christian Science Monitor* diplomatic correspondent Daniel Sutherland, "levels of malnutrition, illiteracy and infant mortality are high even by Latin American standards"—was plagued by the "brutal and at times harshly repressive tactics" of General Anastasio Somoza Debayle's National Guard. Amnesty International reported the "wholesale killing or unacknowledged detention—'disappearance'—of *campesinos* (peasant farmers)," and the "shootings in cold blood of *campesinos* by National Guardsmen, including in one case, the entire population of a village: a total of four men, eleven women and twenty-nine children in the village of Varilla . . . at the end of January 1977." The evidence against Somoza's repressive regime was overwhelming; and Nicaragua would have been a logical place for the Carter administration to show its sincerity in its avowed commitment to human rights. And so it did, in October of 1977, by giving a peculiar Orwellian twist to a policy already mired in double-speak. Carter decided to withold twelve-million dollars worth of economic aid that included loans and grants for the building of rural schools and development of new dietary supplements, while agreeing to send Somoza and his National Guard—the only police and military force in the country—two-and-a-half million dollars worth of military assistance. It was a curious way of demonstrating what President Carter said in his inaugural address was America's "clear-cut preference for those societies which share with us an abiding respect for individual human rights." In the case of Nicaragua, even more so than Korea, Indonesia, and the Philippines, the Carter administration's "clear-cut preference" was for an authoritarian regime which showed little but malicious disrespect for human dignity and freedom.

Even beyond the clear contradictions between rhetorical goals and daily policies the new administration was showing a strong predilection for applying a double standard. A Rand Corporation study released in October 1977* complained that Latin America was "a dumping ground for restrictive and discriminatory U.S. legislation that expresses principles wounded more seriously elsewhere in the world—but too difficult to apply without compromise because of the Soviet threat or some other compelling U.S. national interest." In effect, not much moral fortitude was needed to cut aid to Argentina and Uruguay or stall a loan to tiny El Salvador on behalf of human rights: Latin America as a whole, according to the Rand study, represented only 2 percent of U.S. military assistance grants between 1973 and 1975. But in South Korea, where there were forty thousand American troops, or the Philippines, where the U.S. maintained two major military bases, there was little reason for cutting aid *except* on moral grounds.

Candidate Carter had promised that human rights was to be a moral principle for guiding a heretofore "too pragmatic, even cynical" foreign policy; but for President Carter it proved to be a principle that simply hovered unattached in a rhetorical cloud, waiting to be called into the service of hoary pragmatism. "Wherever the slightest risk has been involved," commented Walter Lacqueur, chairman of the Research Council of the Center for Strategic and International Studies in Washington, "and occasion-

---

*U.S. Arms Transfers, Diplomacy and Security in Latin America and Beyond by David Ronfeldt and Caesar Sereseres.

ally also where the risk involved has been small or non-existent, the administration has tended to retreat from its declared purpose. . . . some foresight and consistency, not to mention a bit more courage, could have been expected."

Carter balked at accusations that his human rights policy was not *policy* but puff, that his outspokenness was little more than symbolism at best, hypocrisy at worst. He seemed to believe, for example, that he was showing the universality of his moral concern by condemning the brutality of Uganda's dictator Idi Amin Dada at the February 1977 news conference where he tried to assure the Russians that he was not singling them out for criticism. "The actions [in Uganda] have disgusted the entire civilized world," he said. But the only thing universal about Carter's condemnation of Amin was the fact that most of the civilized world agreed with him. What would be difficult to explain to the Russians (or anyone else), however, was why the State Department allowed twelve of Amin's air force pilots to enter the United States for helicopter training with an American firm.

Even more inexplicable in terms of a consistent or unflagging commitment to human rights was Carter's warm greeting of the Shah of Iran in November of 1977. His arrival, not surprisingly, precipitated a bloody clash between a crowd of one thousand five hundred well-wishers—many reportedly paid to come to Washington by the Iranian government and friends of the Shah—and a smaller group of hundreds of club-swinging Iranian protesters. The melee in front of the White House left ninety-six demonstrators and twenty-eight policemen injured, some seriously. "Professional agitators," explained the Shah.

Restored to full power in a CIA inspired coup in 1953, Shah Mohammed Reza Pahlavi could hardly be characterized as a ruler that shared with Carter his "abiding respect for individual human rights." He had prohibited any advocacy of communism, attacks on the monarchy or the basic tenets of the political system in all domestic newspapers and journals. All radio and television stations were government-owned. Exiled Iranian poet and professor Reza Baraheni, himself imprisoned for one hundred two days in one of the Shah's dungeons, claimed that "since August 1953, we have been under constant torture." In his account of the Shah's reign, *The Crowned Cannibals* (1977), Baraheni almost matter-of-factly ticked off the statistics of the "terror in Iran": "Thousands of men and women have been summarily executed during the last twenty-three years. More than three hundred thousand people are estimated to have been in and out of prison during the last nineteen years of the existence of SAVAK (The State Organization for Security and Intelligence); an average of one thousand five hundred people are arrested every month. In one instance alone, on June 5, 1963, American-trained counterinsurgency troops of the Iranian army and SAVAK killed more than six thousand people. . . . the number of political prisoners in Iran is still on the rise. The number of announced executions in the first five months of this year (1976) is more than eighty, while the number for the whole of last year was less than forty. . . . There have been occasions when five thousand people have been kidnapped in one day (by SAVAK). . . . The actual army of agents and informants has been reported during the last five years to number from hundreds of thousands to millions."

But though the Shah's jails were reported to hold, according to *Time* magazine, anywhere from twenty-five thousand to one hundred thousand political prisoners, his country's subsoil contained 10 percent of the world's known oil resources. And while the tear gas of the Washington police wafted through the air on that crisp November day, forcing even the Shah to pad his teary eyes with a handkerchief, President Carter spoke of the "wonderful opportunity for us to share experiences," praising the Shah for making Iran "strong, stable and progressive."

By the end of 1977, it had become clear to many that Carter had forsaken his ideals and broken his promises for what Walter Lacqueur called "an aimless and inconsistent pragmatism." He had undermined the support he had appeared to have with America's strongest allies. After the initial flutter of high-minded rhetoric, polls from West Germany showed that his human rights stand enjoyed 79 percent approval; in France, 68 percent. But by the time that the president ended his swirling seven-nation nine-day tour abroad on January 6, 1978, Europeans seemed to have changed their minds. The editor of Hamburg *Morgenpost* and member of West Germany's Parliament, Conrad Ahlers, was calling Carter "the worst political failure of the past year." "Whatever he has touched," wrote Ahlers, a member of Chancellor Helmut Schmidt's Social Democratic Party, "be it the human rights issue, disarmament negotiations, the Middle East, the worldwide recession or the rate of the dollar—he has smashed valuable china." The liberal British daily, *The Guardian,* in offering "a cold, blunt assessment of Carter at this stage," chided the President for "concentrating too much rhetoric on foreign affairs. A man who hymns human rights in February," said the editorial, "should probably not be embracing the Shah of Iran the following December." As Irving Kristol, the Henry Luce Professor of Urban Values at New York University, wrote in the *Wall Street Journal* after fourteen months of the Carter administration human rights muddle, ". . . the rest of the world is at a loss to figure out the relation of what we say to what we mean to what in fact we might do."

Much of the criticism—by now, some of it cynicism—leveled against Carter resulted from the Carter world-wide moral crusade that more often looked like a bad case of situation ethics randomly applied. Not only could the selected victim countries of the administration's human rights campaign point justifiably to the instances of Carter moral myopia whenever traditional U.S. foreign policy interests were at stake (e.g., "national security" in the cases of Korea and the Philippines; arms limitations talks and detente with Russia; OPEC oil and "national security" with Iran), they could also condemn Carter for sweeping his evangelical broom around other countries before putting his own house in order.

There was a certain degree of irony in the fact that at the same time that the State Department embarrassed the president with its 105-nation report on human rights practices, the U.S. Commission on Civil Rights released—with comparatively little fanfare—its summary of civil rights developments in the U.S. during 1977.* Some of the conclusions seemed to make a mockery of Carter's human rights ministrations.

In the section directly comparable to the State Department's analysis of *governmental*—as opposed to the almost undefinable *structural* or *institutional*—abuses of human rights, the "Administration of Justice," the Commission

---

The State of Civil Rights: 1977. A Report of the United States Commission on Civil Rights. Arthur S. Flemming, Chairman. February, 1978. While release of the State Department report prompted a front page story in the February tenth New York *Times,* and a full inside page was devoted to excerpts and related stories, news of the release of the Civil Rights Commission survey three days later was buried in a small article of the *Times* on page twenty-six.

complained of "an increasing number" of reports of "police misconduct, beatings, shootings and intimidation of citizens." The "phenomenon" (an interesting choice of words) is "so pervasive" that in some cities it "appear(s) to be officially sanctioned."

In Philadelphia, for example, said the report, a suspect "was beaten with gun butts and blackjacks by seven police officers and then dropped head first into a parking lot. The victim died as a result. The police misconduct alleged in this case was corroborated by sixteen eyewitnesses, but the matter was never prosecuted. In response to this and other incidents, the United States attorney in Philadelphia began a grand jury investigation of police practices in Philadelphia, and fifteen officers were indicted on twelve charges of brutality and three of corruption." (The U.S. attorney in this case was none other than David Marston, a Republican, removed from his office in January 1978 by Carter under circumstances that brought charges of obstruction of justice against both the president and his attorney general.)

Other "serious allegations" of "misconduct" (the State Department, referring to a foreign country, may have wished to say, "Government failure to enforce proper rules of conduct by the security forces serves to condone brutality. . . .") streamed in from such cities as New York; Houston; Chicago; Los Angeles; Memphis, Tennessee; Jackson, Mississippi; Montgomery, Alabama, "among others." American Indians were an example of a minority commonly subjected to "abuses" that included "setting of excessive bail, refusal to release Indians on their own recognizance . . . illegal arrest procedures . . . physical abuse . . . in police custody, warrantless searches of Indian homes," et cetera. No American Indian, however, was entertained in the Roosevelt Room of the White House by Carter as an expression of presidential concern over abuses of human rights.

When it appeared that Carter might be willing to address the contradiction, he ended up by sidestepping it. In a May 1978 speech at the Los Angeles Bar Association's one hundredth anniversary luncheon, it seemed as if the president would tackle the dilemma squarely when he began by saying, "there is no question that has concerned me more throughout my adult life than that of human justice," citing next his favorite Niebuhrian quotation about establishing "justice in a sinful world," repeating, as he had so often done, that he wanted to carry the human rights message to other nations; and then quickly pointing out that "we cannot speak of human rights in other countries unless we are doing our utmost to protect the rights of our own people here at home."

With such an introduction, one might have expected the president to address such gross violations of human rights as the ones his Civil Rights Commission had said were "so pervasive as to appear officially sanctioned." Instead, he launched an immediate attack on lawyers, showing more concern about economic inequities than human injustices, about delays and timetables than beatings and harassment. Carter said he was "worried about a legal system [not quite the same as system of justice] in which expensive talent on both sides produces interminable delay. . . ." He complained about an excessive number of overpriced lawyers ("We are overlawyered and underrepresented" was the Carter phrase headlined in the next day's press), excessive litigation and, quoting Gandhi, lawyers who "advance quarrels rather than repress them." He carried on about the legal profession as if it were the cause of injustice—an injustice that, in any case, had less to do with illegal searches and seizures or the grosser abuses of officially sanctioned beatings (which Carter didn't mention) than with nettlesome divorce proceedings, title searches on property, simple car accidents, or medical malpractice suits (which he did mention). A speech that began by appearing to promise a forthright analysis of human rights problems in the United States got muddled in issues, however irksome, that often seemed better suited to a lecture on the headaches of small claims courts. In the end, commented the *Wall Street Journal,* "Mr. Carter didn't offer any new suggestions on how to improve the criminal justice system." And as American Bar Association President William B. Spann, Jr., remarked, "it would seem that his basic complaint is with a system that can only be corrected through his leadership."

That leadership was notably lacking when Carter was confronted with the most famous contemporary American case of a violation of human rights, a case to which presidential authority could have been applied much more effectively than was possible with a critique of a group over which Carter had little direct control. (However noteworthy and justified his criticisms of the legal profession, it was, in the end, the diatribe of a campaigner—not a president. Surveys of American opinion had indicated that lawyers were generally not a very respected lot, and with the polls also indicating that Carter's own popularity had reached an all-time low of only 30 percent, only a few percentage points better than Richard Nixon's Watergate nadir, it wouldn't hurt the Carter image to attack an already unpopular group.)*

Less than two months before the LABA address an estimated eight thousand people gathered for one of the largest demonstrations in front of the White House that

---

*There were, of course, exceptions: A resident of Oregon—where Carter, the day after his LABA speech, heaped aspersions on another profession of decreasing repute, medicine—wrote to *Time* magazine, "I would trust my lawyer more than I trust Carter's banker—Bert Lance."

year. Folk singer Pete Seeger was there. Activist Angela Davis told the crowd she hadn't "felt this good in a long time." Voices from a past replete with injustices were that day chanting to yet another president: "Hey, hey, Mr. Peanut Man. What you gonna do about the Wilmington Ten?" It didn't have the cadence or solemnity of a "We Shall Overcome." "Human rights begin at home," they cried. "Free the Wilmington Ten." Jimmy Carter was out of town that day, but he knew of which they sang.

The Wilmington Ten were the most prominent "political prisoners" in the United States. Nobel prize-winning Amnesty International had "adopted" them as "prisoners of conscience" more than a year before the Washington rally, and for almost seven years the group had been a *cause celebre* of civil rights activists across the country. Convicted of arson and conspiracy for the 1971 fire-bombing of a white-owned grocery in Wilmington, North Carolina, following a civil rights protest, the ten (Ann Shepard Turner, the only white person involved, had been released from prison on parole in 1977) had always maintained their innocence. They had been sentenced to a total of two hundred eighty years in prison. Benjamin Chavis, a young black minister, received the harshest term: thirty-four years.

"From the start," said the New York *Times,* "the trial was peculiar. The prosecutor, Jay Stroud, whose conduct throughout became the basis of a petition for a new trial, developed an illness just after selection of a jury of ten blacks and two whites. When he recovered sufficiently to pick a new jury, he got ten whites and two elderly blacks—and a quick conviction." Crucial to the prosecution's case was the testimony of three black witnesses, all of questionable credibility. Two of them were serving sentences for assault with a deadly weapon and armed robbery; and the third was a boy of thirteen at the time of the Wilmington riots. All three eventually recanted their trial testimony, announcing that the prosecution had threatened and bribed them into perjuring themselves for the sake of a conviction. "The police told me I would go to prison for the rest of my life," said Allen Hall, the most important of the three, "if I did not say what they wanted me to say." The youngster, Eric Junious, admitted that Stroud had offered him a minibike and a gas station job in return for his testimony.

On February 2, 1977, the same day that the State Department was forwarding to Carter the letter from Soviet dissident Andrei Sakharov asking the new president for his help in defending other Russians who "struggle for openness, for justice for destroyed rights of other people," Michigan congressman John Conyers and a number of other black leaders were meeting with Carter's attorney general Griffin Bell to plead the case of the Wilmington Ten. Bell, fresh from a near terminal brush with a senate nominating committee that was due to such things as membership in segregated clubs, promised a "very active, high priority" investigation. It wasn't the sky, but at least the new administration seemed sincere in its willingness to proceed quickly.

After a North Carolina Superior Court refused the Wilmington defendants a new trial in May, however, sixty U.S. congressmen wrote to Bell urging him to intercede, reminding him that as a candidate Carter "acknowledged that this case may involve matters so fundamentally unfair as to call for moral and legal intervention by the U.S. He has promised that, if elected, he would 'not tolerate the kind of racist injustice that has so often put civil rights leaders in prison.' In particular he has given his assurance that he would 'give the Wilmington Ten case the attention it deserves.' " They also reminded Bell that a habeas cor-

pus petition—protesting the jury selection procedure in
the original case—had been sitting dormant in a U.S. District Court since February 1976.

The attorney general continued to "investigate,"
though there was some doubt about the height of the investigation's priority. "Justice could have done a lot of
things by now," moaned a Conyers aide in May of 1978,
more than fifteen months after the "very active, high
priority" promise, "but they're simply stalling."

In the meantime, the informal spokesman for the imprisoned blacks, the Reverend Chavis, sent three letters to
the president—the first in March of 1977, a few weeks
after Carter had written to Sakharov promising to "use
our good offices to seek the release of prisoners of conscience," and the third in March of 1978—and received no
response. When asked in April 1978 whether he had considered making even a statement about the Wilmington
Ten, Carter replied, "The *only* thing I have been *willing* to
do is *let* our attorney general investigate the circumstances under which the trial was held. . . . I think it would
not be *appropriate* for me to make a preliminary judgment
from the Executive Branch of government. . . ." [em-
phasis added]. It was odd that Carter couldn't even make a
"preliminary judgment" about the case: he had already
done so as a candidate, and as president his attorney general had presumably been studying the matter for more
than a year. It was also curious that here, in his own country, Carter seemed so hamstrung, reluctant to *allow* (let
alone act as a catalyst for) anything more than an investigation, and was so sensitive to the "appropriateness" of *his*
acting, when he could be so courageous in telling the
United Nations that no nation could "*avoid* its responsibilities" to speak out when "unwarranted deprivation oc-
curs in any part of the world."

After fifteen months in office Carter had retreated from

any appearance of principle in formulating a policy on human rights. He had called the Russians to the carpet for their treatment of dissidents while sending arms to a government (South Korea) he had called "repressive." He had twisted the arms of tiny foreign governments because of their human rights violations while claiming it was "inappropriate" to intervene on behalf of those same principles in his own country. Instead of making human rights "a fundamental tenet of our foreign policy" he had made a mockery of it.

Jimmy Carter's problem as president was not that of a man whose ideals were too great to be achieved. It was that his ideals were frequently only platitudes. They lacked a unifying vision. His morality was often a disparate set of contradictory moralisms connected only by the tenacity with which he held to all of them. As a candidate, the moralisms and platitudes were convincing because of his apparent sincerity. That he campaigned for the presidency promising compassion, love, justice, and competence in government was ennobling—however paradoxical the objectives. That he himself believed firmly in the ethical standards of scripture was refreshing—however subjective his reading. That he spoke candidly of his personal commitment to religion and his desire to make that commitment a moral beacon to guide his presidency inspired confidence in his trustworthiness—however exploitive his self-advertising.

"My impression," wrote the *New Republic's* "TRB" after trailing Carter through his pre-convention campaign speech-making, "is that audiences yearn to believe Jimmy Carter." And believe they did. But Carter and his team of advisors were not country bumpkins in their reading of the popular sentiment. At the same time that Richard Nixon was landsliding the Executive Office aspirations of George McGovern in one of the most lopsided presidential

election victories in the history of the Union, Hamilton
Jordan was drafting a lengthy memorandum for Governor
Carter outlining strategy for a bid on the White House.
"Perhaps the strongest feeling in this country today," Jordan suggested with an amazing degree of prescience, "is
the general distrust of government and politicians at all
levels. The desire and thirst for strong moral leadership in
this nation was not satisfied with the election of Richard
Nixon." Two years later, of course, Nixon had become the
first elected president in history to resign. His most un-
pardonable offense: deceiving the American people.
"When we search out a new president," wrote Carter's favorite political scientist, James David Barber of Duke University, in 1974, "we are looking for far more than mere
professional competence. We want an emotional connection. We want faith beyond works. We want a trustable
hero." And that was exactly what candidate Carter wanted
the voters to have: "They just feel that I'm the kind of
person they can trust." And he elevated it to the preeminent issue of the campaign. An issue that allowed him to
drink from diverse ideological watering-holes; play with
grandiose ideals and moral precepts without dwelling on
the implications of their implementation. "If [the voters]
are liberal," he said, "I think I'm compatible with their
views. If they are moderate, the same. And if the voter is
conservative, I think they still feel that I'm a good president." (A Freudian slip: the election was still eight months
away.)

If the voters hankered after honesty and morality, no
matter what the specific policy—"we want faith beyond
works"—Jimmy Carter said he had the credentials to justify their faith in him. They believed him. "Jimmy Carter
was somewhere within the range of the very good and very
decent man he presented himself to be," wrote Norman
Mailer. And even Mailer thought he would "find himself

on Election Day happy to vote for him: After all, it was not every day that you could pull the lever for a man whose favorite song was 'Amazing Grace, how sweet the sound that saved a wretch like me—I once was lost, but now I'm found, was blind but now I see.' "

Jimmy Carter had sinned; he had been baptized, reborn, and saved. After his conversion and second birth, he personally preached the message of Christian redemption in "foreign" states (Massachusetts and Pennsylvania), inviting others to listen to the word of God, repent, and be saved. "It may seem unjust to punish real religion," commented Garry Wills in the *Atlantic Monthly,* "when we reward empty religiosity. . . ." There had been other religious politicians. Richard Nixon had his weekly White House prayer services; he remembered "vividly" attending an evangelist's revival meeting with his father and two brothers just after he entered high school: "We joined hundreds of others that night in making our personal commitments to Christ and Christian service." Could the voters pass up a sincere Christian after having already cast their ballots for a hypocritical one? Could they not but vote for a man of God who promised moral leadership after having mistakenly trusted a decade and a half of amoral leaders? The whole nation would have to share the guilt for the sins of Vietnam and Watergate, shoulder some of the blame for Richard Nixon and the Bay of Pigs and the Chilean coup. Jimmy Carter promised to help purge the nation of its sins.

As he campaigned for the presidency, he constantly moved from criticisms of past administrations to subtle rebukes of the American people. In announcing his candidacy, he blamed government for betraying our trust. Yet two sentences farther on he was blaming a collective malfeasance for the sins of the past: "The purposes and goals of *our* country are uncertain and sometimes even suspect."

It was not Richard Nixon or the CIA or the government that was suspect, but "our country." Though his standard stump speech called for a "government as good as its people," he just as easily implied that the people themselves had not measured up: "You want to see us once again," he told a black audience in Florida, "have a nation that is as good and honest . . . as are the American people." It was the nation that had faltered, not the government. "I hope we've learned some lessons," he chided a Kentucky gathering a month later. "One lesson is that we should cease trying to intervene militarily in the internal affairs of other countries. . . . We lost thirty-four thousand in South Korea and fifty thousand in South Vietnam."

Few speeches appealed to this collective sense of guilt more than Carter's triumphant acceptance of the Democratic nomination: "We have been shaken by a tragic war. . . . Our party has not been perfect. We have made mistakes, and we have paid for them. . . . We feel that moral decay has weakened our country, that it is crippled by a lack of goals and values. . . . We have been a nation adrift too long. . . . Our country has lived through a time of torment." Somehow, Jimmy Carter seemed to say, *we* must repent for *our* sins—for the tragic war, our imperfections, mistakes, the moral decay, the absence of goals and values—and place our trust, like children, in a leader who is moral, religious, who himself has repented and been saved.

The voters decided to accept the flagellation as a rite of purification. Carter's moral premise was not so much that the American people were good and decent as it was that they had sinned but were still capable of being saved. When it came time to formulate political policies and make political judgments, however, the salvationist politics practiced by President Carter were full of contradiction. "There has always been this puzzle about Jimmy Carter,"

wrote veteran New York *Times* political columnist James
Reston after fifteen months of the new administration,
"—whether the smile on his face or the chip on his shoulder would prevail. He has been trying to play the game
both ways, being very moral on one hand, and very clever
and political on the other. . . ." It wouldn't work, said Reston, and Carter "is discovering that there is a fundamental difference between how to win an election and how to
govern after you win. . . . If he is going to serve 'the general interest' and rely on the judgment of the people, he
cannot defend Bert Lance one day, and raise the
minimum wage the next, proclaim 'human rights' in the
Soviet Union and South Africa and Rhodesia, and ignore
them in South Korea and the Philippines for strategic reasons. This is a fundamental political and philosophical dilemma for Jimmy Carter, even a theological question,
which he hasn't yet resolved."

First, however, Carter would have to factor out the
weirdo factor: distinguish what was politics from what was
philosophy from what was theology. The struggle between
the "smile on his face" and the "chip on his shoulder"
aggravated everyone but Jimmy Carter. What others saw
as a "puzzle" was no puzzle at all for a man who looked at
religion through a glaze of political precepts and saw government as God's earthly arm; thought the world to be
more an image of himself than he of it, a welter of infinite
complexity, unpredictable, answerable only to itself and its
God. "I'm not a packaged article that you can put in a little
box," he would say. "I have different interests, different
understandings of the world around me, different rela-
tionships with different kinds of people." He challenged
people to understand him, defied their attempts to do so,
and was elected before anyone realized how little substance there was to his differentness.

III

The Media

*I don't know. Sometimes I think people look too hard. They're
looking for something that isn't there. I don't really think I'm
that complex. I'm pretty much what I seem to be.*
—Jimmy Carter

Jimmy Carter perhaps had nothing better going for him as
a candidate than the fact that he was a politician in the
instant-image age of electronic journalism. A made-for-
television candidate, he benefited as much from the
medium—and the media—as it from him; a man as eclec-
tic and fleeting and transparent as the images which
floated endlessly by the hour across television screens.

There was a kind of natural symbiosis between Carter
and the press, a give and take of mutual concern and
shared goals. It had less to do, as McLuhan had taught,
with the message than the medium; less to do with *what*
Carter was than *how* he was; less to do with the specula-
tion about whether he resembled John Kennedy or had
the sex appeal of Robert Redford than with how the Carter
campaign and presidency mimicked so well the nightly
news.* Carter seemed able to change positions with the

Time magazine artists were reportedly once instructed to draw a portrait of Carter that looked as much like J.F.K. as possible. But for all the
attempts at conjuring up some sort of lusty machismo that would make
women swoon, Carter seemed never to get farther than the sexuality of
an Ultra-brite toothpaste commercial.

same rapidity and dexterity as Walter Cronkite on a given evening could leap from terrorist attacks in Southern Lebanon to the Dow Jones Industrial Average.

One day Carter's top economic priority was jobs; the next, inflation; and then on yet another day, it was a combination of both. He would argue adamantly for the necessity of a fifty-dollar tax rebate, winning the support of the AFL-CIO and key members of Congress, then drop the proposal without warning. On September twenty-first he could remember the exact date when Bert Lance told him of a Justice Department investigation and by October twenty-ninth not recall ever hearing of it. Or at one point in a press conference he could go on and on about how little he knew about the removal of Philadelphia's U.S. attorney:

> I have recently learned about the United States attorney named (David) Marston. This is one of hundreds of United States attorneys in the country and I *was not familiar with the case until it became highly publicized.* The attorney general is handling the investigation of the replacement for Mr. Marston ... and *I've not interfered at all.* ... We have encouraged ... the Democratic members of Congress not to be involved in trying to influence the attorney general about who should be the new United States attorney there. ...
> *I've not discussed this case with the attorney general.*
> [emphasis added]

And a little later in the same press conference he was admitting that he *was* "familiar" with the case before it became public. He *had* "discussed" the case with his attorney general and even ordered him to "expedite" Marston's removal. He *had* "interfered."

By almost anyone's standards, there was something fishy

about the turn-abouts and obvious deceptions. But Carter
was slipperier than most, possibly betting on the possibility
that the public memory was as long as yesterday's nightly
news, a media event which had less to do with what was
said than how it was said and by whom (Barbara Walters
wasn't earning a million dollars for her expertise in domestic and foreign affairs). It seemed to have worked for Carter, at least while he was campaigning, adapting as he did
to the electronic media which catapulted him to national
prominence. In a certain sense he became part of it. Carter was a medium from which information flowed, not so
much like a granddaddy river, deep and wide, as like a
gurgling, rampaging whitewater stream, splashing quickly
over and around every protrusion. Like the scattered bits
of ninety-second news stories that were lumped together
for no other reason than that they were "news," Carter
could tick off the disconnected fragments from his *cur-
ricula vitae* for no other reason than to say that he, quoting
Kierkegaard, was an "exception" just like everyone else: "I
am a southerner and an American. I am a farmer, an
engineer, a father and husband, a Christian, a politician
and former governor, a planner, a businessman, a nuclear
physicist, a naval officer, a canoeist, and, among other
things, a lover of Bob Dylan's songs and Dylan Thomas'
poetry." Did that prove that he was an exception like
everyone else, or that he was simply like everyone because
he had done everything. The more bits of significant yet
unexplained information transmitted, and the more often
they came, the less possible it became to assemble them
into a coherent whole, the less time and inclination to
wonder about the past,or issues, or contradictions, or deceptions. Who could remember what Walter Cronkite had
said two days before? The best memory was of Cronkite
himself, monotonously and transparently, yet honestly,
one supposed, ticking off the day's horrors.

There was something about Jimmy Carter that yearned to imitate the soothsayers of television news who were able to monitor the world's pulse without being a part of the seedy events. Polls had often shown Cronkite to be the most trusted man in America. The wizened, level-voiced, sober and experienced television commentator could be counted on to tell it like it was, and communicate the facts without bias. He was an unblemished window on the world, and no matter how absurd and contradictory or painful were the facts, he reported them. He remained clean. And his integrity was not judged by the rush of events that he reported but by the way he did the reporting.

That was how Jimmy Carter wanted to be judged: not on issues or ideology, but on his ability to be a barometer of events. He portrayed himself as the unblinking, unbiased eye of the camera; he zoomed in on the nation and replayed the action. "To travel around this nation," he continuously and characteristically exclaimed, "to meet American people, to talk a little, to listen a lot, to receive questions and suggestions and expressions of the hopes and dreams of two hundred fifteen million of us is . . . always educational." He wanted to *travel* and *meet* and *listen* and *receive*. It was not Jimmy Carter traditional politician that the voters were going to elect: it was the Walter Cronkite of politics. "I hope I have a chance to exemplify what the American people are and what they would like to be."

Gerald Ford was waging his campaign from the cozy surroundings of the White House Rose Garden, signing important documents of state, smiling for the television cameras, using the power of the incumbency to attract the media but not the sympathy of the mass audience. It was old-school politics, superannuated since the days of Richard Nixon who came to believe that an isolated president could actually control the levers of power.

Jimmy Carter said he knew otherwise. He was the populist *par excellence,* telling the people (all of them) that he was one of them, not one of the special interests, the big shots, the decision-makers who were "isolated from the citizens" and maintained their power by means of secrecy and deception. Like the mass media (only better) which followed him around, Carter was the supreme democrat, the great leveler who would put people in touch with one another and bring them once again to Washington. "I'm an outsider, and so are you," he continuously said. "Watergate has made outsiders of us all." "Watergate" was a buzz word for secrecy and dishonesty. And an "outsider" didn't describe a geographical state as much as a communicative one. "I'd like to form an intimate relationship with the people of this country. And when I'm president, the country will be ours again."

Richard Nixon, perhaps, came to hate the press because it was a constant reminder of the fact that the real power resided somewhere beyond him; and he fell in disgrace because in part the press finally *exposed* him. A major turning point in the domestic battle over the Vietnam war was the *revelation* of the Pentagon Papers; just as the *public testimony* of CIA chief William Colby and the *reporting* of journalist Seymour Hersh threatened the spy establishment.

In revivifying the tired and worn cliche about the power of public opinion, Carter was able to remain one step above the issue itself, talking about it without touching it.

He eventually called the Vietnam war "racist" but only after it had become politically acceptable to do so. If anything, while the war was raging, Carter was a closet hawk. But it was interesting to follow him through an explanation of his handling of one of the most controversial issues of the previous decade and a half. In his *Playboy* interview he admitted that he "never spoke out publicly about with-

drawing completely from Vietnam until March of 1971"
(not, however, because he thought the war was *wrong*, but
because he believed it a "mistake" to fight without the intention of winning), and even then only because "it was the
first time anybody had asked me about it. I was a farmer
before then and wasn't asked about the war until I took
office." (Actually, Carter couldn't have been as innocent
and naive as his "I was a farmer" statement, seemed to
suggest. "From 1966 to 1970," he wrote in his autobiography, "I worked with more concentration and commitment than ever before in my life. I tried to expand my
interests in as many different directions as possible, to
develop my own seed business into a profitable and stable
enterprise, and to evolve a carefully considered political
strategy to win the governor's race in 1970.") Then Carter
characteristically began talking about the climate of public
opinion at the time. "There was a general feeling in this
country that we ought not to be in Vietnam to start with."
And the fact that the people had been duped: "The American people were tremendously misled about the prospects
for victory. . . . If I had known in the sixties what I knew in
the early seventies, I think I would have spoken out more
strongly. I was not in public office." Carter seemed to be
saying that he had no personal feeling about the war, that
his stand (or lack of it) depended on "a general feeling in
this country," which he couldn't really express until he was
a public official. Even when *Playboy* pressed him about
what his own views were, Carter replied, "There was an
accepted feeling by me and everybody else that we ought
not to be there. . . . and I might hasten to say that it was the
same feeling expressed by Senators Russell and
Talmadge—very conservative southern political figures."

Eight years after Lyndon Johnson had abdicated because of the turmoil over Vietnam and a year after the
United States had finally admitted defeat, and Jimmy Car-

ter still could not bring himself to a declaration unsupported by the "general feeling," or the "accepted feeling," or the "same feeling expressed by Senators Russell and Talmadge." Carter always had his ear to the ground, listening for the general will, waiting to know what the people thought.

For Carter, Vietnam didn't have so much to do with right and wrong as with winning and losing; and ultimately with the fact that he and the "American people were tremendously misled." It seemed to be in the deception, the lack of candor and communication, that the real evil of Vietnam was perpetrated. Carter himself could go either way on the issue of right or wrong. His instincts were more democratic than moral: he wanted to give people what *they* wanted; monitor the "general feeling" and then do or say what the representative of that feeling should do or say.

That attitude, if extrapolated into a theory of political action for the executive office, was to a certain extent a brief for presidential impotence. Carter had sketched such a role for himself—for any president—almost from the time that he began campaigning. A president could do no more than be something of a nightly newscaster, a witness to events, not their master, and hope only to be a good communicator.

In a revealing passage from *Why Not the Best*, Carter recalled his introduction to Tolstoy's *War and Peace*, the Russian novelist's classic account of the mechanisms of historical progression. His high school teacher, Miss Julia Coleman (who was later memorialized by Carter in his inaugural address), had suggested the book to Jimmy when he was twelve years old, and he remembered being "happy with the title because I thought that finally Miss Julia had chosen for me a book about cowboys and Indians." As Carter found out, it was not.

He goes on to give a brief synopsis of *War and Peace*. "The course of history was changed as great men struggled for military and political power. But the book is not written about the emperor or the czar. It is mostly about the students, farmers, bankers, housewives, and common soldiers." Carter himself was then struggling to become one of the "great men" of history as any president of the United States was bound to be. But, as Carter explains, "the purpose of the book is to show that the course of human events—even the greatest historical events—is determined ultimately not by the leaders, but by the common, ordinary people. Their hopes and dreams, their doubts and fears, their courage and tenacity, their quiet commitments determine the destiny of the world."

Carter said that *War and Peace* was one of his favorite books and had even read it "two or three times since then" (no small undertaking). And what he learned from it and how he applied it was most interesting for a man who had planned so assiduously his path to leadership. "If the author were correct in his claim that the destiny of nations is controlled by the people, even when they are ruled despotically by kings and emperors, how much more true should this be in a nation like ours where each of us is free! Our government is supposed to be shaped and controlled by the collective wisdom and judgment of those among us who are willing to exert this power and democratic authority. But often those who want no special favors from government do not participate actively in the political process."

In this light, the Carter candidacy seemed not so much a populist manifesto as a crusade to accept the inevitable dictates of history. Jimmy Carter, the man who wanted an "intimate relationship" with two hundred fifteen million Americans, was to be the representative of "the collective wisdom" of the people. All he had to do was convince a plurality of the electorate that he could somehow institutionalize the thesis of *War and Peace,* be a "great man" who willingly bowed to the will of Everyman, who knew what that will was.

The problem was that all the populism in the world was of little use to a candidate who was unknown to the people (accepting for the moment that Carter's populist claims were legitimate). As both an "outsider" and an unknown, Carter had to cut a lot of corners to win a place in the White House. He had to be some sort of political magician to form that intimate relationship in so short a time. The popular upheaval had to be somewhat contrived.

Only a handful of people, and that limited to a few million residents of Georgia, knew him in 1972 when he first decided that he would run. His formal declaration of candidacy in December of 1974 was attended by only a faint whisper of recognition from the press. But even then he was sounding Tolstoy's trumpet: "I have learned a great deal about our people. I tell you that their great dreams live within the collective heart of this nation." And the press would soon begin listening to the man who seemed to be saying exactly what it was supposed to be doing: telling the people about each other. Eventually, Carter the outsider got his biggest boost from one of the most powerful of insiders. The multi-billion dollar media establishment gave Jimmy Carter what he needed most: recognition and a platform. And in the way that was most beneficial: short-hand communication, quick sketches, sign language. The press gave Carter an instant image.

If he had to pick up any establishment support and at the same time try to cultivate his anti-establishment image, the press was the best power-broker to go to. It was a near monolithic establishment that portrayed itself as a friend of the people. Who, after all, lit the fuse on the bomb which eventually blew Richard Nixon to political oblivion? The press seemed to live in the same democratic floodlight of public approval that Jimmy Carter wanted so much to bask in. For a decade and more the media had played the role of intermediary and catalyst in the cause of openness. Journalism schools were bulging with aspiring young investigative reporters in the wake of such "outsider" demolition jobs as *The Pentagon Papers* and *All The President's Men.* Television had bloodied cozy living rooms with color footage of a real war and put millions of lounge-chair people in touch with thousands of shouting street demonstrators. Liberal white northerners by the hundreds had hopped in cars and trains and buses bound for Alabama after seeing fat white policemen turning firehoses and raving dogs on groups of weaponless blacks. If, as Carter learned from Tolstoy, "the course of human events . . . is determined ultimately not by the leaders, but by the common ordinary people," then it seemed that the press had been instrumental in bringing the ordinary people together—or at least giving that impression—thus hurrying the course of human events along. The candidacy of Jimmy Carter was one of those human events that got a substantial shove from the media.

But the press was anything but an impartial window on the world. It itself was not a part of the common weal however much it appeared to espouse the popular sentiment. "The media present a democratic image," wrote Sheldon Wolin, Professor of Politics at Princeton. They seem to be "the vehicle for making culture accessible to all without appearing to impose any elitist standards." Wolin believed television "particularly beguiling" because it gave the impression that it transcended the normal workings of the marketplace where *caveat emptor* was the golden rule. "No transaction is immediately evident; there is no symmetrical exchange of things, no reciprocal satisfactions, no self-interest, no power transferred. It conveys the impression of offering something of value," said Wolin, "at no cost to the viewer and with no visible gain to the purveyor."

Carter fit this conception well, not only as the candidate who represented himself as a spokesman for the populist mentality ("a media code word for democracy" according to Wolin), but as an outsider who claimed to be running a no-strings-attached campaign, promising governmental love, compassion, honesty and justice that required—trust me"—no *caveat emptor*. He presented himself as a sincere and candid communicator. It was "a basic truth about presidential politics," he believed, "that one does not pursue the presidency by high oratory but by plain talk, not by talking down to people but simply by talking to people, directly and candidly." He didn't believe in intermediaries. He was not going to speak "for the entertainment of the press corps"; he would talk to the people so that they could "judge me on an informed basis."

It was an image much like that which the media cultivated about itself—a promise to involve the people in the events (the facts, the truth?) as if they were *actually* on the scene themselves. It was like the bold two-page newspaper ad for ABC news which announced that its "anchor people" were now going to be "out there closer to the news" imparting important information "from a perspective you only get from *being there*." Frank Reynolds would be in Washington to "add scope and understanding" to coverage of the "national arena"; Max Robinson would be in "the heart of America—Chicago" to "better reflect the interests and concerns of a majority of American viewers" (or as Jimmy Carter would say, "I can represent what our people are and what we want to be and what we can be."); Peter Jennings would be in London "to better assess the meaning of each (overseas) situation"; and in sum, ABC's World News Tonight would give "a clear, concise, comprehensive narrative of each day's events. Wherever the news is, if humanly and technologically possible, we will be there. And if you turn to ABC so will you." Jimmy Carter said he was "out there" and promised that if the electorate turned to him, Washington would be out there too.

In fact, the media, like Jimmy Carter, were anything but the "democratic image" they portrayed themselves to be (according to Wolin, Carter would become, in the presidency, nothing more than "a public caricature of plain democratic values"). Wolin's succinct description of what the media actually were bore a striking resemblance—in more than metaphor—to what the Carter candidacy and presidency turned out to be. The media are, "first and foremost," said Wolin, "an industry which rests on an enormous investment of resources and skills; and as in all modern enterprises, decisions are taken on a highly self-conscious basis with a studied regard for their implications and effects. Second, the media are dispensing a commodity (news, entertainment) which is produced not so much to be consumed or used but to have an effect on what people do and believe. Third, the media are closely connected with the public opinion and survey industry so that a closed circuit effect is created: the pollsters *nee* market analysts feed back to the media the results of the latter's manipulations so that future programming can be improved; i.e., later polls will confirm the success of the program."

In sheer financial weight alone—aside from how that weight was put to the task of imparting news—the premier media companies were as well-rooted in the "system" as a General Motors or Exxon; and those at the top of the communications heap enjoyed a prestige and power that was purchased and sustained by dollars and capital not votes.

Time and *Newsweek* not only had a virtual monopoly on

the weekly general news readership market in the country, they were each a part of a wide-ranging and lucrative corporate enterprise. Time, Inc. controlled the country's largest cable television company, owned seventeen weekly newspapers, book publishing companies, timberland and lumber products companies, and investment companies—all together giving it a healthy standing among the nation's top industrial corporations. *Newsweek* was owned by the Washington Post Company, which also controlled radio and television stations, book publishing companies, and a news service for other papers around the country. (To tighten the capital's media belt a bit more, Time, Inc., in 1978 purchased the city's only other daily newspaper, the Washington *Star*.) As for television, there was little doubt about the corporate strength of the big three: NBC was owned by RCA, the thirty-first largest company in the country; CBS racked up sales of $2.2 billion in 1976; and ABC kept pushing farther ahead of its competitors in the Nielsen ratings. Add the New York Times Company, and the Times Mirror Company (the Los Angeles *Times*), numbers 394 and 232 respectively on the 1976 Fortune 500 list of the top companies; the huge chain-stores of newspaper land, Gannett and Knight-Ridder, each with a long list of communications subsidiaries in every part of the country; and the remaining "independents" who for the most part turn to the Washington and New York giants for their national news; and with no trouble at all the press in the United States could begin to look about as outsiderish as Nelson Rockefeller. Media was big business that just happened to have a reputation—deserved or not—for being something of an anti–big–shot big–shot. It was also the last of the giant corporate contributors, other large donators having been virtually excluded from the campaign process by the new ceilings placed on cash contributions.

Not that the media trundled trunksfull of cash out of closets to drop on a candidate's doorstep. In fact, what direct dollar flow there was went in the media's direction—not the candidate's. "Each camp in 1976," said Jules Witcover of the Ford/Carter contest, "budgeted about half the federal subsidy (of $21.8 million alloted to each candidate) for the media, and nearly all of that amount for paid television." But that television time was augmented many times over by the hundreds of hours of free publicity showered upon the candidates and fed to the public as news. "Engineering 'free media' became the highest political art form," observed Witcover, who had trekked after the candidates as a reporter from beginning to end. "Getting the candidate on the network evening news was the *sine qua non* of each day's plan; everything else revolved around that objective. The bare arithmetics of campaigning in the television era—obtaining street crowds numbering tens of thousands at the very most, with perhaps a hundred or so actually shaking the candidate's hand, as opposed to the millions watching Cronkite or Chancellor or Walters—was overwhelmingly persuasive."

The media were in the business of selling news and the candidates were in the business of selling themselves as news. This mutual dependence made it difficult to determine exactly who benefitted more from whom, who mimicked whom in the round-robin circus of winning votes and reporting the news. There was no more memorable moment in the televised Ford/Carter debates (except perhaps the president's painfully memorable remark, "There is no Soviet domination of Eastern Europe . . . .") than when the sound equipment went dead for twenty-seven full minutes during the candidates' first live, face-to-face encounter. For almost a half hour the television audience saw two human appendages of modern electric circuitry. As the cameras were left trained on the two candidates for almost the entire breakdown, both Ford and Carter stood transfixed as if frozen in ice, unwilling or unable to look at one another or speak to one another or even sit down. They reacted to the mechanical breakdown as if the electronic capacitor which died was their own; and one hundred million Americans were treated to the sight of two grown men—leaders of men—acting like wooden soldiers who hadn't as yet been visited by the fairy godmother.

If the media at times seemed to lead the candidates around, it was by no means a one-way street. For the reporters who followed the candidates around the country, filing their daily or weekly reports for the executives at home, being on board the plane or bus of the winner could mean a large step up the career ladder. Ken Auletta, a staff writer for the *Village Voice* in New York asked a few Carter campaign reporters about the potential conflict of interest and received responses that sounded much like a politician's evasive non-response. Stanley Cloud of *Time* magazine said, "That's a good question. I have had no promises from anyone at *Time*. I suppose if Carter wins I will become White House correspondent. I view that with mixed emotions. I suppose I wouldn't turn it down. Obviously, the thrust of the question is does it affect one's coverage? I think not, because I'm not all that enthusiastic about going to the White House in the first place." However mixed-up Cloud's response, his mixed emotions about going to Washington were immediately clarified after the election: he was offered the job as White House correspondent, and he took it. James Wooten of the New York *Times* was riding the fence on the matter, in much the same way as his candidate: "There is a distinct possibility I may be asked to go to Washington. My inclination at the moment is no, I don't want to go to Washington. On the other hand, there are strong arguments. I'm forty years old. Maybe it's time to stop running around the country." Wooten may not have wanted to go to Washington, but he didn't turn down a White House correspondent's position when it was offered. Curtis Wilkie was only thirty-six and hadn't been with the Boston *Globe* for very long before he joined the Carter campaign press entourage. He too claimed he didn't want the Washington assignment, though he was candid about the advantages of the job: "I'm going to be in a position to actually know a president and a vice president and be able to say to my kids, if they win, that I covered probably the most remarkable political story of this century. The political thing to do is say it doesn't matter. Shit, it does . . . . If he sees me he'll know who I am. No president ever knew who Curtis Wilkie was." The thirty-ninth does, and Curtis Wilkie will be able to tell his kids about stepping through the White House gates almost every day for the special briefings given to the White House press corps.

The most overt example of the suspiciously close ties between candidate Carter and the press was a remarkable advertisement for *Time* magazine, circulated nationwide just prior to the New Hampshire primary. Distributed in the country's leading periodicals—e.g., *People, Sports Illustrated, The Atlantic, Harper's, Chicago, Smithsonian, New Times, Texas Monthly, Forbes, San Francisco, the National Observer*—it was ostensibly intended to boost the magazine's reputation as an upbeat and incisive purveyor of important political news. In fact, as *Harper's* editor Lewis Lapham remarked with considerable understatement, it "looked very much like an ad for Jimmy Carter."

Centered dramatically on the full page which the ad covered was a large photo of Jimmy Carter, serenely posed, á la John F. Kennedy, in a high-backed wooden rocker, one foot propped casually against the banister of what looked like an unpretentiously home-spun front porch (actually the Georgia governor's mansion). Above the photo, in large bold-face type was a quotation (evidently from one of *Time's* political correspondents) which read, "His Basic Strategy Consists of Handshaking and Street-Cornering His Way Into Familiarity." (If a picture was worth a thousand words, this ad was probably worth a million handshakes.) The caption below the photo read, "Jimmy Who? That derisive question was often asked in Georgia when the peanut farmer first ran for governor in 1966. But not when he made it on his second try in 1970." A full two-thirds of the advertising page purchased by *Time* was devoted to "Jimmy Who?" the "handshaker and street-cornerer" (i.e., a man of the people) overcoming "that derisive question" on his way to inherit the legacy of Camelot (the handsome young man poised for action yet possessed of the wisdom of the elders). Only if the reader ventured to the fine print at the bottom of the page would he be told that—ahaa!—Jimmy Carter was really only "the subject of a capsule biography, one of a series exclusive in *Time* . . . *the* weekly news magazine." Not so curiously, however, no other candidate was used in *Time* advertisements to hype its "series" on the candidates. Even Carter campaign headquarters would have been hard-pressed to match the expert Madison Avenue techniques that *Time* employed on behalf of the former Georgia governor.

Not surprisingly *Time* denied any gratuitous political hanky-panky. And the magazine could probably be taken at its word. There was no need for any secret conspiracy or back-room deal between Carter and media executives; no under-the-table cash tendered in exchange for future political favor. The connection was both more simple and more subtle than that: in effect, pretty pictures sell candidates for president as well as they sell the news; and when you're in the business of selling news about candidates, why not use a pretty picture of a photogenic candidate who's newsworthy?

The press, in its dual role as the Christopher Columbus of politics and the Simon Bolivar of the power-elite, found in Carter a reservoir of potential journalistic wealth. He attracted a slurry of journalists out to discover the secret of the mysterious dark continent of a politician. And in finding a solitary man preaching on street corners and in factories and schools about the latent power of the people, they helped raise the banner of the underdog and banish the "derisive question."

The New York *Times* sent Norman Mailer, literary hero of the March on the Pentagon, to Plains, and titled the ensuing report as if he had gone to El Dorado: "The Search for Carter." The author of *Armies of the Night* responded appropriately, beginning his Carter travelogue, "Plains was different from what one expected," and left his readers with a reverential and sentimental discovery: "Yes, he was quiet in charisma, and no massings of energy rose like thunderheads from his brow. You could come near him in a room before you were aware he was there. Nonetheless, his aura was hardly the same as other people's. Happiness came off him. It was as if he knew that God had given him intelligence and good work that would make sense, and so he could give his strength to the world and get new strength back. The emotional heat of the heart might be free of the common bile."

If Normal Mailer was converted, Hunter S. Thompson was born again. "Once the mad-dog Prince of Gonzo, the drug-soaked cynic who four years ago wrote that Big Bad Ed Muskie was strung out on Ibogaine," said Thompson colleagues Michael Drosnin and Ron Rosenbaum, ". . . suddenly endorsing a faith-healing peanut farmer for president . . . . Hunter Thompson blissed out on Jimmy

Carter." For two years Thompson had carried around with him a tape-recorded speech of Carter's, the Georgia Law Day Speech of 1974, playing it for anyone who would listen. "It was a king hell bastard of a speech," wrote the thunderstruck journalist recalling that day. "It was sure as hell not what [the audience] had come there to hear." Thompson was converted.

Jimmy Carter was full of mystery and surprises and contradictions, and the press loved it. Journalists from Gonzo Fear and Loathing Hunter Thompson to rough and tumble Norman Mailer jumped on the magical mystery ship. Periodicals from hip *Rolling Stone* to pithy *Time* to serious New York *Times* all flocked after the rumored mother lode. The *Times* dubbed Carter the "1976 Surprise" before 1975 had ended. From the early, early days of the campaign to its closing moments, headlines and subtitles continually marched Carter before the public—in itself a sign of kudos from the press—dressed in the outsider's robes of enigma. "No candidate has been so extensively covered," wrote Garry Wills after it was all over, "yet so ill described." But the mystery seemed part of the package. "A Southern Democrat In the White House?" wondered the *New Republic* as early as April 1975. "Jimmy, We Hardly Knew Ya'll," said *Playboy* as late as November 1976. Carter was always the puzzle to be solved, just as Plains for Mailer was "different from what one expected," or his Law Day Speech for Thompson was "sure as hell not what [the audience] had come there to hear." Carter was "The Yankee from Georgia," or "Just Like the Rest of Us Only More So." He offered "McGovernism Without McGovern," or "The Well-Planned Enigma." There were fact-sheets on "Engineering the Politics of Love," "God and the 1976 Election," and "Reading the Carter Riddle." If the only record of the 1976 campaign were the fleeting images left by the headline writers, future electoral archeologists could very easily conclude that American voters in 1976 didn't have any idea who it was that they chose to lead them.

One thing the Carter camp knew long before it began crisscrossing the country in its "lonely" search for votes was that its most important big-league support would have to come from the press. No inside power-brokers could be enlisted to promote the candidacy of a man trying to "develop the image of a highly successful and concerned former governor of Georgia and peanut farmer living in a small rural town," as Hamilton Jordan described the Carter persona in 1972. In the early planning stages for the assault on Washington, the Georgians worried about "generating favorable stories in the national press," "developing a proper image," "developing . . . a close personal relationship with the principal national columnists and reporters."

While Hamilton Jordan's 1972 strategy memo revealed some naiveté about the manner of gaining press acceptance, it more importantly suggested a highly sophisticated respect for the media establishment that in more traditional political times might have been reserved for big city political bosses, union officials, wealthy financiers, party leaders, or big business. "There exists in fact an eastern liberal news establishment," wrote Jordan. It had "tremendous influence" and "could establish you [Carter] as a serious contender." Jordan suggested making a list of editors and columnists "who you know or need to know. You can find ample excuse for contacting them—writing them a note complimenting them on an article or column and asking that they come to see you when convenient." Jordan could just have easily been talking about presidential power-broker George Meany, boss of the powerful AFL-CIO; or Richard Daley, symbol and master of efficient machine politics. But instead he advised Carter:

"Some people like Tom Wicker [columnist for the New York *Times* and its Washington Bureau chief] or Mrs. Katherine Graham [owner of the Washington Post Company] are significant enough to spend an evening or a leisurely weekend with . . . ."

Despite Carter's insistence that he would cull no favors from special interest groups—"I have never asked for endorsements. My whole effort is to go directly to the people themselves"—he was, in fact, developing plans to win the endorsement of the Fourth Estate. Such an endorsement, as Jordan well knew, would come in the form of "recognition and acceptance of your candidacy as a viable force." If big labor liked the record and political philosophy of Senator Henry Jackson, the media could make the peanut farmer from Georgia an instant superstar; and even teamsters liked superstars. The Carter people weren't embarrassed by the label, even after the election. "We've got the biggest star in television," said an ebullient Barry Jagoda, Carter's television adviser, after the Georgian had been in office for a few months. "Jimmy Carter may be the biggest television star of all time."

"The strategy was to get to know the press," said Atlanta ad man Gerald Rafshoon, the media man for the Carter campaign. "We knew your names," he told journalist Ken Auletta, "even if you didn't know ours." It was Rafshoon who had given Carter a copy of Tim Crouse's *The Boys On The Bus*, a who's who insiders account of the reporters on the 1972 campaign trail. The governor read it twice, and "everyone," recalled Rafshoon, "who worked with us in early 1974 and 1975 read Crouse's book." By the time of the first electoral tests of his candidacy, Carter was well-versed in the mechanics of press manipulation, and that knowledge was used to turn little wins into larger-than-life media victories.

His team worked diligently in Iowa, the kick-off state in

the presidential campaign game, even though the state would contribute only forty-seven of the more than three thousand convention delegates. Carter "knew Iowa was this year's New Hampshire," commented Frank Mankiewicz, Robert Kennedy's 1968 press secretary, and the little tussle there "was unlike the National Football League, where game fourteen can count as much as game one." The national press would be there to magnify the results into a mini-referendum of national significance.

In late October 1975, almost three months before the actual precinct caucuses, Iowa Democrats gathered for their annual Jefferson-Jackson Day dinner. All the major presidential candidates attended, the national press was there, and the Des Moines *Register* and *Tribune* decided to poll the participants about their candidate preferences. Carter campaign organizer for Iowa, Tim Kraft, who "knew the thing was going to be covered," knew also that "politics is theater" and "planned for that." He packed the crowd as best he could with Carter supporters, suggesting that they wander down to the gymnasium floor and appropriate any loose ballot sheets they could find. He even advised Carter sympathizers to paste bumper stickers on whatever they drove to the event because "there's usually a reporter who polls the parking lot and throws a sentence in about it."

The strategy paid off. Not because Carter won the largest percentage of votes in the straw poll, but because he wound up two days later on the front page of the New York *Times* (the newspaper that Jordan saw as the preeminent member of the eastern liberal news establishment, "the best paper in the country and possibly the world") described as having "taken a surprising but solid lead" in Iowa.

By the time Iowa Democrats went to their 2,350 precinct caucuses on January nineteenth, CBS news commentator

Roger Mudd was candidly admitting on national television that "it's not exactly the precise figures that will be important, it's whether or not the media and politicians agree that this man won and this man lost . . . . During the night it will be the collected wisdom, or misjudgment of the media and the politicians that's going to determine who actually comes off well out here." So much for letting the voters decide.

Mudd was entirely correct. Carter polled 28 percent of the vote, but the "uncommitted" slate won with 37 percent. That didn't stop Mudd from going back on the air the next day to report to the nation that Jimmy Carter was the "clear winner." "No amount of bad-mouthing by the others can lessen the importance of Jimmy Carter's finish . . . . The Iowa results caused the Carter campaign overnight to grow a long tail of newsmen."

During the next month, Carter lost three of the five state precinct caucuses, but after Iowa the press had focused on the first real primary on February twenty-fourth, in the tiny state of New Hampshire. There Carter won a slim victory of six percentage points over Morris Udall, but the press didn't see it that way. Both the national weekly news magazines rushed out cover stories and *Time* took the occasion to run a long idyllic biography of this "proud Southerner" who was "not satisfied with just peanuts" (which, not so coincidentally, came right on the heels of their national advertising campaign on behalf of "Jimmy Who" and their political reporting).

"Jimmy Carter," said *Time*, "has been the surprise and irritant of the politics-as-usual world." But the real surprise was that with only a few thousand votes from the first small primary election counted and Carter only barely a winner; with millions left to be polled; with the convention still months away; and with still almost fifty primaries and caucuses to be waded through, *Time* declared the still unknown former governor "a leading contender for the Democratic nomination."

The press loved drama. The unknown, the underdog, the outsider, offered a chance for exploration; and the temptation to be the first to shout "Eureka! I've found it," the future president, the "leading contender" was too great an opportunity to pass up.

Occasionally there were gentle reminders from inside the ranks of the media about the basics of democracy: "A good rule to remember," said CBS reporter Bruce Morton before the primary season had begun, "is: the fella with the most votes wins." But rarely was that rule remembered as the oracles of the political press gathered after each session of democratic muscle flexing to explain what had *really* happened and what it meant for the future; how candidate X, who had received 26 percent of the vote, had scored a moral victory over candidate Y, who had 28 percent, because candidate Y was expected to do much better than he did and candidate X had not made much of an effort in this state and was expected to place a distant third at best, et cetera.

If not quite adhering to the democratic rule, the press and the candidates had their own, which worked rather effectively for the Georgian: call a spade a club often enough and loud enough and soon everyone will be seeing clubs. Jimmy Carter seemed to be the ill-begotten club that the press early on began calling a spade. "Carter's disadvantage," wrote Robert Shrum, "was suddenly a supreme advantage: he was the unknown to be explored, the mystery man to be identified, while the rest of them [Udall, Bayh, Jackson, Harris, et al.], familiar faces to the press, simply couldn't compete for publicity."

Even when Carter was running face to face against Ford, who was known on the press plane as Bonzo (Carter was referred to as Weirdo), he received the advantages of media shove. The televised debates, for example, seemed less popular than the news analyses which followed them and some polls suggested that the post-debate commentaries were an important factor in deciding audience response. A Notre Dame psychology professor, Dr. Lloyd Sloan, ran a test in which he monitored the reactions of three different groups to the debates. One saw only the October sixth debate, and, according to Sloan, registered "an overall shift of 20 percent in favor of Ford." The other two groups, however, saw the debate *and* the commentaries which followed on CBS and ABC; and in those groups Sloan noted a remarkable change. "After the debate itself had its positive impact for Ford, the network news analyses by themselves produced overall net changes of 27 percent (CBS) and 22 percent (ABC) in the direction of Carter. Those who viewed the post-debate analyses saw both as being biased in favor of Carter."

Television, perhaps more than any other branch of the media, seemed notoriously capable of helping the democratic process along. And Jimmy Carter, of all the candidates, gleaned the most advantage from its weaknesses and biases. "Television news," commented Paul H. Weaver, an associate editor of *Fortune* magazine, "likes a man who can be presented as having genuinely been raised up out of obscurity by the people alone. He emerges as the good guy on the nightly news."

Weaver knew something of the subject: every night during the entire primary season he watched television's evening news programs; and with the aid of a university videotape system he studied each program a second time. He concluded that television news was anything but the window on the world of modern folk media lore. Reporters and commentators alike repeatedly passed judgments and had few qualms about passing them on to their audience. But not just as simple declarative statements. Television more often showed its biases in the act of creating for its viewer, in the course of a few minutes reportage, a complete and comprehensible world that didn't mirror the real one so much as caricature it. After his many hours of watching and rewatching television news, Weaver believed that it was "not primarily information but narrative; it does not so much record events as evoke a world. It is governed not by a political bias, but by a melodramatic one . . . . The diversity, complexity, and uncertainty of the real world become all but invisible. They are replaced by the false simplicity and clarity of what television news, assuming a posture of omniscience, pretends to know, in sharp detail, about the politician's every important action, secret hope, fear, plan and motive. Instead of participating in a long, confusing and often inchoate political process, as he does in the real world, television's politician acts out a clear and gripping melodrama—call it "The People's Choice."

Jimmy Carter became a principal actor in the melodrama because, as Weaver pointed out, he "was lucky enough and clever enough to exploit the biases that are built into the practice and definition of television news." Carter "understood, and derived benefit from, television's myth of the politician. In running against Washington, he was in fact running against a political image that television helps to perpetuate."

So it was that television—in much the same fashion as print media—called Carter's slim victory against four opponents in the New Hampshire primary a "substantial victory" but would only grant Henry Jackson "a strong finish" when he captured 23 percent of the vote in Massachusetts with seven opponents a week later (Carter finishing a distant fourth). "What is there about Carter's twenty-three thousand votes" [all he got in New Hampshire], asked Weaver, "that merits a lot of respectful talk about his 'momentum,' whereas Jackson's one

hundred and sixty-three thousand votes [in Mas-
sachusetts] elicit little more than surprise? The answer is
that there is no justification for these distinctions;
Jackson's win in Massachusetts was at least as important as
Carter's in New Hampshire."

Carter's was a much more melodramatic story to tell: an
obscure, one-time Georgia governor, battling against the
entrenched political power-brokers, promising never to lie
or mislead, or carry on in any way like the politicians of the
previous decade, and claiming to know both the will of
God and that of the American people. It was a much more
digestible tale than complicated analyses of complex issues
could ever hope to be.

Television executives would complain that the medium
wasn't always capable of in-depth analysis. "We just can't
handle issues the way a newspaper can," said Richard Kaplan, a producer for CBS Evening News with Walter Cronkite. "A writer can go into all kinds of detail to explain
things. We have to have something on that film. And
you've got ninety seconds to tell it."

But they also pointed out that candidates weren't all that
interested. As Kaplan, who was assigned to the Carter
campaign, pointed out, Carter would use television's limitations to his own advantage. "What do you do if Carter
says the big issue is who you can trust? We were in a terrible predicament. We were stuck . . . . We were interested in
issues, but Carter couldn't say how he would reorganize
the government. He couldn't even say whether you were
going to have to pay more taxes."

For all the help that he received from the media's free
lunch program, Carter had to protect himself from accusations that he was avoiding controversial issues or was
an intentionally "fuzzy-on-the-issues" candidate. Sometimes he tried to "defuse" the problem with sleight-of-
hand image manipulations reminiscent of the tactics of the

political type that he said he was running against. After Carter had barely managed to squeak by Morris Udall in the Wisconsin primary in April, winning by a narrow one percentage point, his ears-to-the ground pollster Pat Caddell heard rumblings of voter discontent over the issues issue. Caddell's post-election survey turned up "two disturbing notes" which struck at the heart of the Carter campaign thrust. "First," reported Caddell, "the leading Carter negative on open-ended responses was the category 'not specific, wishy-washy, changes stands,' which went from 3 percent in our first poll to 11 percent in the last survey. Also, the agreement to the projective statement 'Jimmy Carter always seems to be changing his positions on the issues' rose from 23 percent in survey one to 33 percent in survey two." Something had to be done, he warned. "We must defuse the 'no specifics and changes positions arguments.' They seem to be rising. And inevitably unchecked lead to perceptions of Carter as 'untrustworthy' and 'dishonest.' "

Media adviser Rafshoon immediately went to work defusing the charge. Onto existing television spots for Carter he simply tacked on a new introduction and conclusion. "Jimmy Carter on the issue of . . . ." was the new lead; and "If you see this *critical issue* the way Jimmy Carter does, then vote for him." In effect, there had been no clarification of the issues; only a statement saying that they were clear.

Another tactic was to usher in the press as a scapegoat. ". . . the national news media have absolutely no interest in issues *at all*," he told *Playboy* as the problem nagged him into the campaign against Ford. "There's nobody in the back of this plane who would ask an issue question unless he thought he could trick me into some crazy statement." Rarely had anyone "tricked" Carter into saying something "crazy"; though he often made contradictory and confusing statements, the most notorious ones as he wandered away from a reporter's question. In fact, his craziest statements—"I've looked on a lot of women with lust. I've committed adultery in my heart many times .... I don't think I would *ever* take on the same frame of mind that Nixon or Johnson did—lying, cheating and distorting the truth"—were made (in the *Playboy* interview) while giving a rather lengthy and roving response to the question, "Do you feel you've reassured people with this interview, people who are uneasy about your religious beliefs, who wonder if you're going to make a rigid, unbending President?"

The press itself sometimes engaged in a bit of self-criticism for its contribution to the vacuousness of public debate which preceded the general election. In a special post-election section of the *Columbia Journalism Review* James McCartney took the media to task for its appetite for "junk news," but the problem was more one of a chicken-or-the-egg variety. "Never was so much that meant so little presented in such technologically perfect fashion to such a widely yawning public," said the Knight Newspaper Group's Washington correspondent. A good example, said McCartney was a Carter speech in New York on October fourteenth in which the candidate outlined his proposals for a strategic arms agreement with the Soviet Union, calling for a "quick freeze" on the number of atomic missiles and warheads, on total "throwweight" (i.e., destructive power), and "qualitative weapon improvements." McCartney complained that this important "new approach ... in a field involving not only the life or death of the nation but of civilization itself" was not even mentioned by the New York *Times* in its story about the speech.

Curiously enough, however, when Carter had a chance to set the record straight, he himself opted for a non-controversial past. When he published a book of his campaign speeches after the election (*A Government As Good As Its People*), he devoted three pages to that October fourteenth speech and left out any reference to either the Soviet Union or strategic arms agreement proposals. Not so curiously he left in his familiar platitudes about a foreign policy that should concern itself with "real wisdom rather than imagined toughness," about losing "trust in our government," about the two hundred fifteen million Americans who are the "greatest resource of all," et cetera.

Jimmy Carter spent a great deal of time and money convincing the electorate that he was a trustworthy populist. But in flying over the normal complexity of the democratic process, by spurning the grand domos, the machines, the ideologues, the party leaders, the special interest groups; by selling an artificial image of himself to a media establishment which instantly and hourly flashed like a neon billboard nationwide, Carter ultimately trapped himself, became either a slave to the passing fancies of popular whim or an easy target for those who froze the action to look closely beyond the language of symbols. Even if Carter had the best of democratic intentions, he would suffer because of his belief that the media were a democratic institution. The same media which catapulted him to the White House, would savage his presidency. His celebrity status would wear thin: the Nielsen ratings would eventually reveal him as the overnight star whose light faded after a single season.

The first storm began to break over the Carter clean image campaign as it geared up to take the nation by surprise in the Iowa caucuses and New Hampshire primary. On the morning of January nineteenth, the big day in Iowa, the New York *Times* ran an article which summarized some of the recent criticisms of Carter. It pointed out, however, that "the most searching criticism is yet to come in the March issue of *Harper's*." No nationally distributed periodical had yet taken Carter to task for the exaggerated and deceptive picture he had painted of his record as Georgia governor. And the rumors that were circulating among journalists and insider politicians was that the *Harper's* piece would be "something big." In fact, the article would become "something big" before it was even published, and then more because of the Carter camp's desire to head the horses of skepticism off at the pass than the article itself.

The chronology of events was an important factor in what ensued. On January thirtieth, more than two weeks before Steven Brill's article was scheduled to hit the newsstands, Carter's press secretary Jody Powell called *Harper's* editor Lewis Lapham to request an advance copy. After extracting from Powell a promise that the article would not be circulated, only used to prepare a response when it finally appeared, Lapham complied.

On February second, however, Powell came forward with a long and detailed attack on Brill and rebuttal of the reporter's charges equal in length to Brill's as yet unpublished article. The press secretary at the same time handed out copies of the original article to selected reporters.

On February third, Jimmy Carter announced on television that an upcoming *Harper's* article was "very, very vicious . . . full of outright untruths . . . the most remarkable piece of fiction I've ever read." At about the same time, according to Lapham, the magazine began to receive phone calls and letters from people purporting to be longtime readers aghast at the magazine's unseemly demeanor in printing such an article (which was still unpublished). A phone call to one of the letter-writers by a suspicious Brill was answered by a man at Carter campaign headquarters in Atlanta. Lapham decided to release the article late that day.

As the rest of the nation's press began to pick up the

story, Carter's first-attack tactics were beginning to pay off:
the issues raised by Brill had been relegated to second-class
news in deference to the honest campaigner's claim that he
was being slandered. Columnist Jack Germond of the
Washington *Star* on Februrary fourth characterized the
article as a "liberal assault on Carter perhaps unmatched
in harshness and intensity in any presidential campaign of
the post-war period." *Time* magazine on February ninth
quoted an unnamed Washington reporter calling Brill "a
hit man ... the liberal enforcer" in an article heavily
weighted with attacks on Brill and titled "Doing a Job on
Jimmy."

It shouldn't have been too surprising that the Carter
camp reacted with such speed and hostility to Brill: the
article tread unceremoniously on the heart of the Carter
image. Brill claimed that the Georgia governor was running "the most sincerely insincere, politically anti-political,
and slickly unslick campaign of the year. Using an image
that is a hybrid of honest, simple Abe Lincoln and charm-
ing, idealistic John Kennedy, he has packaged himself to
take the idol-seekers for a long ride." The title that editor
Lapham gave to the story was no less consoling for the
man who promised over and over again that he would
always tell the truth: "Jimmy Carter's Pathetic Lies." That
in itself raised the hackles of Carter sympathizers.
(Lapham later made a backhanded concession, admitting
that the word *pathetic* may have been "imprecise. *Beguiling*
might have been more accurate, or, even better, *welcome*. I
had not thought that so many people still wanted to believe
in the image of a hero, even an image so grotesquely
exaggerated that it bordered on parody.")

In the article Brill zeroed in on the discrepancies between what Carter was and what he was saying he was.
Carter, in his 1970 Georgia gubernatorial campaign
against former governor and liberal Carl Sanders, said

Brill, had mounted an attack that implicitly appealed to the latent (if not overt) racism of the Peach State population, courting such notorious segregationsists as Roy Harris, organizer of the White Citizens' Council. Brill quoted a man who had worked in the campaign and told him of a Carter "stink tank" operation which had distributed a racially disparaging anti-Sanders leaflet and secretly funded radio ads for black gubernatorial candidate C. B. King, the one man who could woo the black vote away from the front-runner Sanders. Carter's claims on his record as a government reorganizer were contested; his attempts at covering over his hawkish support of the Vietnam war and George Wallace were detailed; and a miscellany of various Carter deceptions and issues waffling. It was no wonder that the Carter camp wanted to manage and contain the Brill article; and in the short run succeeded in much the same way it engineered its campaign: As he ignored the traditional support lines of organized politics so that he could deliver his well-planned public image to the people through a medium with which he was intimately familiar, he attempted to short-circuit *Harper's* (and short-change the public?) by writing the scenario for the public before all the actors were on the stage.

What made the affair so surprising, however, was that Brill and *Harper's* were not alone in their criticisms of Carter, but they were the only ones that the Carter camp chose to attack. On February seventeenth the Associated Press sent out a story by Dick Pettys which disputed Carter's claims about his success at reorganizing the Georgia bureaucracy (with even more damaging detail than Brill had supplied). The Washington *Post* followed on February twenty-eighth with a story headlined "Carter's Claim of Cutting Bureaucracy Disputed," with further evidence in support of Brill's contention that "whatever good Carter did do as governor is blurred now by the legend he is trying to make of it." The Miami *Herald* on the same day not only affirmed Brill's account of disreputable tactics that Carter had used in the gubernatorial campaign but also revealed a number of instances where Jody Powell had compounded the duplicity in his rebuttal of Brill. Both the Washington *Post* and the Detroit *News* weighed in on March seventh with more evidence of "dirty tricks" in the 1970 Carter campaign. There was no twenty-two-page rebuttal of these articles, despite (because of?) the fact that they were, for the most part, more detailed in their criticism and more damaging in their evidence.

What the Carter strategy seemed to have been was pick off the first major critical article that would receive a national reading (i.e., *Harper's*), steal it, condemn it loudly before anyone knew its contents, crying foul, "vicious," and untrue, thus gaining press attention that would divert the public gaze from the issues that were raised. It seemed to have worked. By the time that "Jimmy Carter's Pathetic Lies" finally arrived on the newsstands on February seventeenth, the Carter machine had already created a different story. And when *Time* ran its long praiseworthy biography of Carter in its March eighth issue, it brushed aside the evidence undermining his credibility with the assertion that "Now that he is a real challenger, Carter is being asked to pass sterner tests than other candidates." It did concede that Carter "has been accused of fudging the issues. He has been charged with telling little white lies — and indeed he has occasionally exaggerated past accomplishments — along with some big ones." What were his "little white lies," his exaggerations, his "big ones"? *Time* didn't say.

The quickness with which the Carter forces mobilized — it took two days to write a rebuttal which equaled in length a story that Brill had spent months researching — indicated how well prepared they were to deal with the charges when they surfaced. Most of what Brill had said, in fact,

had been known in Georgia political and journalistic circles since the 1970 campaign. Brill just happened to be the
first one to try to bring Carter's real record to the attention
of a national audience. And he was dexterously manhan-
dled by an experienced team of media manipulators.

Candidate Carter managed to block the swipes taken at
his fabled and romantic past by combining a sophisticated
sensitivity to the press process with a well-planned, organized, and fast-paced campaign. He had a "detailed interest in the inner workings of the press" reported Sanford
Ungar of the *Atlantic Monthly,* "more so than any presidential candidate since John F. Kennedy. He is familiar with
deadlines, and understands the difference between what
will make news in a small town and what on the national
level."

Carter had his detailed seventy-page strategy memo
from Hamilton Jordan in hand by late 1972, two years
before he announced his candidacy, four years before the
election. Earlier that same year he had finagled his way to
the podium of the Democratic National Convention to
nominate Henry Jackson for president. According to Jody
Powell, part of the reason was to gain national television
exposure, an admission that may have resulted (a) from
the fact that Carter was running *against* Jackson in 1976
and couldn't afford to appear overly sympathetic with the
senator's consistently conservative political philosophy,
and (b) because he may have wished to draw attention
away from the fact that he had — at the same time that he
was nominating Jackson — tried to maneuver for the
vice-presidential spot on the McGovern ticket. His campaign schedule for 1975 had been planned to the day—
two-hundred and fifty of them on the trail — and abided
by with near perfect precision. In 1974 he had pulled
down the job as chairman of the national Democratic
Campaign Committee, traveling the country ostensibly to

promote his party's mid-term candidates but making sure that he met as many people as possible and that they would remember him. He visited with newspaper executives and reporters. (The day after his 1974 Law Day Speech, he had Hunter S. Thompson over to the Governor's mansion to eat some grits and watch the Kentucky Derby on television.) He decided on his basic stump speech before most of the candidates had even convinced themselves to run. Pollsters had given him careful readings of the populace, and by the time he began his formal campaign all the important non-issue issues were formed. "I said certain things over and over, day after day, month after month," he explained and then repeated them again: "That government can be both competent and compassionate. That America's foreign policy should reflect the character of the American people. That we could have, and must have, a government as good as its people." He planned carefully for the early primaries and entered almost every state race. "The Carter campaign," said Robert Shrum, "was a fast train along the primary track." And for much of the press, the requirements of filing frequent reports on the latest developments often allowed little time for the type of substantive and analytical reporting that Steven Brill did.

"During the campaign," CBS correspondent Bob Scheiffer later recalled, "we were so burdened with spot news — all the little horse-race stories — that issue stories got swallowed up. It's not that past performance stories weren't done: they just got overshadowed." But it probably wouldn't have mattered anyway, Scheiffer added. "I think what it came down to was that people just wanted an outsider. This election was really just the last chapter of Watergate."

Even James Wooten, a man whom the Georgians eventually forced out of his job as White House correspondent for the New York *Times,* saw the fickle finger of fate writing the scenario for 1976. "I doubt that if the entire press corps had set out early on to destroy Carter — which, of course, it did not — that it would have succeeded. He was the perfect candidate for 1976."

How so? "Take for instance a part of Carter's persona like his hometown background," the deposed reporter explained, giving, perhaps, one of the more succinct of summaries — if not very complimentary toward the mentality of the American electorate — of the 1976 election. "You had to write about it. Who is this Jimmy Carter? Well, he's just this fella from down here in Plains, Georgia. Where's Plains, Georgia? Well, it's one-hundred and forty miles southwest of Atlanta and has a population of seven-hundred and fourteen. What's there? Nothin' much there. Jimmy's pretty successful in this little town. People respect him; some people dislike him; but they all kind of admire him because of his hard work and what he did with his daddy's business there. His mother's kind of eccentric, but fairly interesting. His brother is crazy, but fairly interesting. His wife's a dud, but what do you expect.

"In telling that story, which was pretty impossible not to do, whether on television or in the New York *Times* or in the Waukegan *Journal,* it was precisely to Carter's advantage. Even writing about it in a sneering kind of way was to Carter's advantage . . . . And if you're going to insist that the people of this country didn't know that Jimmy Carter was a rather specious candidate, there's not much I can do about it."

Wooten was no neophyte observer of political power exchange. This was the third presidential campaign he had covered. He joined the Carter press contingent before there was much of one — in December of 1975 — and prior to that had been the *Times'* Atlanta bureau chief in Georgia. He was considered one of the best political reporters that the *Times* had; and, among the many journalists tracking Carter during the campaign, Wooten had the reputation of being the best writer.

Still, if there were some things that a journalist "had to write" about Carter, there were other things that Wooten would have liked to write but couldn't. The *Times* probably would have considered "not fit to print," a Wooten comment at the Democratic Convention overheard by journalist Richard Reeves: "I sound like I admire the Carter people; actually I despise them. I know he doesn't believe that religious stuff. I know it! I know it! Southerners know he isn't a good ole boy or poor — he's the patrician of the town. His language is so subtle and smart. He thinks he's 99 percent smarter than anybody who's around him. He has no respect for scribes; he hates the press."

"I wanted to write that there were very few things Carter wouldn't do to promote his candidacy," Wooten later recalled with a more professional candor, "but that's a subjective judgment ... easily challenged by Jody Powell or Jimmy Carter or Ham Jordan because it would have been like trying to prove a negative."

Wooten, nevertheless, succeeded on a number of occasions in reporting news which infuriated the Carter camp. In March of 1976 he picked up a revealing inconsistency in one of Carter's stump speeches. It seemed that in ticking off a list of American heroes, Carter would always mention the old standbys like Washington, Jefferson, Lincoln, the Roosevelts, Truman and Kennedy; but the name of Martin Luther King, Jr., earned a place in the litany only when Carter spoke in front of black audiences. White audiences wouldn't know that Carter thought the slain civil rights figure was an American hero. Wooten approached Carter with the discrepancy and asked the Georgian if he'd "forgotten" about King.

"No, I didn't forget," said Carter abruptly. He then told the reporter, "I won't do it again."

When Wooten wrote about the incident, he noted the whites-only omission and left the impression that Carter changed his pitch with the audience, that, perhaps, Carter was a politician like all the others. He also mentioned the candidate's promise not to repeat the mistake, which carried the obvious implication that Carter himself admitted that he had been duplicitous. The story did anything but endear Wooten to the Carter camp.

Later in the campaign, while Carter was losing ground to Gerald Ford, Wooten touched another sensitive Carter chord: his indecisiveness. When it was discovered that FBI director Clarence Kelley had received three-hundred and thirty-five dollars worth of government carpentry work in his home, Carter seized the incident as if it were a Watergate-in-the-making — especially since Ford had decided not to dismiss Kelley. "When people throughout the country, particularly young people, see Richard Nixon cheating, lying, and leaving the highest office in disgrace," proclaimed Carter, "when they see the previous attorney general violating the law and admitting it, when you see the head of the FBI break a little law and stay there, it gives everybody the sense that crime must be okay. If the big shots in Washington can get away with it, well, so can I." It was a trivial variation on an old theme, a tilting at windmills. Nevertheless, Wooten decided to ask Carter the obvious question: if he were in Ford's shoes, would he fire Kelley? "Yes, I would have fired him," said Carter. A little later Wooten asked Carter the next obvious question: Will he fire Kelley if he wins the election? The candidate wasn't sure about that.

When Wooten wrote his account of Carter's hedge, he pointed out the "apparent contradiction" between the two statements; and in doing so, as he later recalled, sent the Carter camp "right up the wall. I got quite a bit of crap from Powell then."

But if Carter hated any suggestion that he was like the rest of the brood of politicians, or that he covered up his waffling indecisiveness with high blown rhetoric, he positively stonewalled at the hint that he resembled the all-time political scheister himself: Tricky Dick. "Equating Carter with Nixon makes Carter so mad that he becomes more like Nixon," commented Washington journalist Aaron Latham.

That was something of what happened when, three months into the new administration, Carter enjoying a honeymoon 75 percent popularity rating in the polls, the New York *Times* ran a front-page story entitled "Carter's Style Making Aides Apprehensive." The byline read James Wooten. Even though Wooten chose to compare Carter with his mentor, Admiral Hyman Rickover ("Like Admiral Rickover, Mr. Carter can be . . . brutally brusque and sharp-tongued with those who displease him or disagree with him"), the portrait Wooten sketched of the thirty-ninth President recalled a much more sinister presence in the Oval Office.

> The President tends to cling to his power, to intimidate subordinates and to be ill at ease with strong-minded assistants who dissent . . . . The effect of such an approach in the White House seems to have touched even such long-time aides as Jody Powell and Hamilton Jordan . . . . More and more the president seems to be retreating into the sanctuary of his little study, emerging to speak 'to the people' . . . but stepping further and further away from the people he gathered together to help him govern . . . . Mr. Carter had shown a mounting jealousy about his power and his responsibilities.

The White House was not pleased. And it reacted with a quick fury that eventually brought more attention to its weaknesses and sensitivities than to the Wooten story. Press Secretary Powell was making early morning inquiries of the White House staff, "going straight down the list," to track down the leaks — Wooten having given his sources the privilege of anonymity. By nine o'clock, having no luck at ferreting out the traitors, Powell called Wooten and challenged the reporter to reveal his sources. Wooten declined.

A few hours later, at the daily briefing for the press corps, Powell was asked to comment on the Wooten story. Instead of a simple denial, he fumed on for a half hour, condemning Wooten, denying everything, including being "uptight about the thing." At one point the press secretary said, "You know, the one thing that I don't do, and that I hope I never get into the position of feeling like I have to do, is trying to race around trying to find out who said this or that to a reporter." A few moments later, however, while attempting to prove that Wooten's story was based on the observations of unnamed sources, Powell said he knew that the nine senior staffers had not talked to Wooten and there were "about twenty" other staffers "that I had a chance to touch base with" that morning.

"You actually asked twenty people if they said that?" asked one incredulous reporter. "Did you expect them to say yes?"

However damaging the *Times* story itself may have been, it was the White House reaction to it that drew the most attention — Carter later called Wooten the Erica Jong of reporters. Unlike the Carter team's managing of Steven Brill's blast at the idyllic image, however, it lost the advantage of first strike, and the seriousness with which Powell went about claiming that it was not true only reinforced the impression that it probably was.

The White House was by no means defenseless. Carter and his staff had long memories and they forgave slowly. During the campaign they had their "enemies" list of pressmen who weren't reporting the party line. In June of 1977, *Harper's* was not among the forty magazines which the Carter press office regularly reviewed for the president. The White House refused to give the New York *Times* an interview with the president—the only prominent newspaper so treated—until it had finally succeeded in forcing Wooten off the beat in March of 1978.

"My piece appeared on a Monday (April 25, 1977)," Wooten recalled much later. "Charles Mohr [the *Times'* other White House reporter, and also in ill favor] and I were scheduled for a sit-down interview with the president on Friday. It would have been the first *Times* interview with the president. Well, we never got one until Martin Tolchin and Terence Smith took over the beat (some eleven months later). And their first day on the job they were ushered into Jimmy's office for a sit-down interview." Such is the power of the presidency. "It's really a closed circle."

Wooten believed that he incurred Oval Office anger only because his "Carter's Style" story was "the first kind of hard-assed piece" about "Carter as a president who was not exactly Little Jimmy Sunshine . . . . They'd had a free ride from November second on; and they were a little bit surprised and shocked that anybody would write tough about James Earl Carter, Jr. I mean, My God, he's a wonderful fella, he's a fine man, he's a great president, he's going to save the country from itself. How could you do this? That was an attitude that was encouraged by the fact that they'd been coasting downhill for a long time. And they just froze me out after that — a favorite tactic of White House press operations . . . . My paper did not really respond with any great heroic posture on it; my paper took me off the beat. On the premise that I was not as effective as someone else might be. I couldn't quarrel with the logic, but I sure as hell debated the principle of it. I never said that the New York *Times* caved in to the White House. The White House just locked the door."

The timing of Wooten's uncomplimentary story about the reclusive and rigid man behind the folksy facade marked a turning point in the Carter presidency. Still riding the wave of popular symbolic gestures — the inaugural march down Pennsylvania Avenue to the new home, a fireside chat, teaming up with Walter Cronkite for a telephone call-in from the people, entertaining a Soviet dissident, a town meeting in Massachusetts, a television special on a-day-in-the-life-of-Jimmy — Carter rode into the spring of his first year enjoying a favorable rating from some 75 percent of the population.

Then began the long slide. Like the Mississippi, Carter began flowing slowly and consistently south.

By late November of 1977 he had fallen farther in the polls in the first ten months of office than any of his five immediate predecessors except Gerald Ford. By the spring of 1978 he had reached a point that was only a few percentage points better than Richard Nixon at his worst. Edward Kennedy was outpolling Carter as the Democrats' choice for their 1980 candidate. Even Georgians, who had given their former governor his biggest victory margin in 1976, were expressing their concern over the president's ineptness, his inconsistency, waffling, broken promises and appearance of being too small a man to handle the job. Only 44 percent gave Carter a favorable rating. The Atlanta pollster who conducted the survey, Claiborne Darden, Jr., was warning his candidate clients in the South that they "not get Carter involved [in their campaigns] under any circumstances." Dr. Edward Renwick, director of Loyola University Institute of Politics as well as a consultant and pollster, said in June that in Louisiana "only one out of three voters gives him a positive rating." "It was a close state for him at the height of his popularity," said Renwick. "Now he couldn't carry this state if he were the only name on the ballot." By late May of Carter's second year in office, the polls indicated that Carter couldn't beat Gerald Ford in 1980.

Things looked a lot different from the inside; but from

the outside, the inside looked pretty much the same, just more out of control. "Jimmy Carter," observed Wooten, "is a man both capable of and guilty of obfuscation, being devious, purposefully confusing issues, saying one thing on one hand and something else on another, dealing from the bottom of the deck, and using every technique that every other president in the modern era of the presidency has ever used . . . . The real difference between Carter and other presidents in this regard is that he's not very good at it."

On April sixteenth and seventeenth Carter called the top officials of his beleagured administration to a two-day strategy session at the presidential retreat at Camp David, Maryland. All agreed that the biggest problem the administration faced was selling their programs to the people. The president's advisers called on Carter to bolster his image by getting out among the people, travel more, do what he did during the campaign.

"Jimmy Carter is still a remote, distant figure to many Americans," said the ever-vigilant pollster Pat Caddell. "After fifteen months in office they are still not sure who he is."

So Carter went back on the campaign trail. There were just two differences: he was an insider, not an outsider; he was the president, not the candidate. He traveled to several western states in early May, pledging more solar energy money in Colorado, denouncing the elitist legal profession in California and attacking money-hungry doctors in Oregon and Washington.

He summoned to the White House his old campaign media adviser from Atlanta, Gerald Rafshoon, offering him fifty-six thousand dollars a year for, as Rafshoon said, "developing the themes of the presidency and getting them out."

It seemed to be a strange diagnosis of the problem,

though consistent with the Carter style. He had been the candidate who was called something of a media wizard, a "natural" on television, a man whom the voters (the television watchers) immediately empathized with, and who, in the early stages of his administration, as Richard Reeves observed, "can seem to do no electronic wrong." Bob Scheiffer told Reeves that "Carter's White House operation is about the same as the others, but these people are more clever. They know when it's to their advantage to be helpful to us. Like the joint swearing in of an anti-war guy (Sam Brown, director of Action) and a disabled Vietnam veteran (Max Cleland, head of the Veterans Administration). You know you're being had, but you do it exactly the way they want it done because they're right, it's good television."

The president of NBC News, Richard Wald, added, "There is a difference with these people. It's not that they are doing things that differently than Nixon or Johnson did. It's that they are a new generation and they're less troubled by doing it. They take manipulating television for granted."

Carter had been "on the record" more than any president in recent memory. He had been faithful to his promise of a press conference every two weeks. He constantly invited out-of-town journalists to the Oval Office for exclusive interviews. What was Carter's problem? It was really Carter, not Rafshoon, who was supposed to "develop the themes of the presidency" and he had had (and created) more opportunities to "get them out" than most of his predecessors.

The president "is profoundly misled," warned a normally sympathetic Tom Wicker of the New York *Times*, "if he believes the press is responsible for his low public standing, or that it can be improved substantially and for the long term by a better White House public relations effort."

Wicker chided Carter for ignoring the substantive political realities — as opposed to the quite different "media politics" — of an office whose effectiveness depended on "mediating among interest groups, cultivating their support, orchestrating the strongest combinations of forces in Congress, timely and effective mobilization of public support, gauging what the traffic will bear." "In fact," Wicker concluded, "Jimmy Carter's record so far suggests the danger inherent in the era of media politics: candidates who get elected primarily by their successful use of television and imagery may not have, or may gain too slowly the skill and experience necessary to manage the political offices they have won. And the danger is doubled when such candidates arouse expectations that cannot be met by political performance."

Carter, it seemed, was in the process of rewriting a biblical admonition: The candidate who wins by the television, shall perish by the television. Or as Richard Reeves put it, "Whatever his technical mastery of the monster, it is not his medium — because Jimmy Carter is not a nice man. Nice people, in general, do not get to be president of the United States. . . . The more Carter speaks, the more he exposes himself on the screen — no matter how impressive his content and style — the more risk he takes that people will come to know and understand him. That is not to his advantage."

In fact, in one sense Jimmy Carter *was* known by the populace. As a candidate he was their image; he mirrored "the hopes and dreams of two hundred and fifteen million" of them; he was an outsider (like everyone), a populist (for everyone), a farmer (for the natural man), an engineer and planner (for the technocrat), a born-again Christian (for religionists), and a lover of Bob Dylan's songs (for Hunter S. Thompson). It didn't even matter that Carter was really not any of those things in the way that anyone imagined. What mattered, eventually, however, was that *he* believed he was all of them. He was no less enamored of the image than the people who voted for him.

One book that was studied by the Georgians was Tony Schwartz's *The Responsive Chord*. Schwartz was a respected New York media consultant who had developed hundreds of commercials for Coca-Cola and was brought into the closing stages of the campaign to do the same for Jimmy Carter that he did for soft drinks. "Whether it's Coca-Cola or Jimmy Carter," said Schwartz, "what we appeal to in the consumer or voter is an attitude. We don't try to convey a point of view, but a montage of images and sounds that leaves the viewer with a positive attitude toward the product regardless of his perspective." What for Candidate Carter were the blessings of an image which conveyed a "positive attitude" without a "point of view" or "perspective" ("I'm not an ideologue"), for President Carter became the trauma of execution. The presidency demanded leadership, not fickle mimesis. To the extent that Carter believed all the stories he told about himself, he was indeed what he seemed to be — which in the campaign meant being a man for all reasons, and in the presidency meant trouble. In the acting out of the illusion he paralyzed the Oval Office.

IV

A Man for All Reasons

Jimmy Carter was never one to restrain his hyperbole when the situation demanded it. No matter the facts—his point always seemed to go beyond the facts, stretching somewhere off into the horizon where the sun was aglow with promise and goodness and change.

He could stand before the delegates to the National Democratic Issues Conference on a November day in Louisville almost two years before the election and decry America's despicable lack of respect for the people of other nations. South Korea had responded in kind by "kicking us in the shins to demonstrate some superficial independence of us." South Vietnamese governments were constantly overthrown "as they became acknowledged to be American puppets." And then a volley of recrimination to sum up how unAmerican American foreign policy had become: "When I go into an embassy in South America or Central America or Europe and see sitting as our ambassador, our representative there, a bloated, ignorant, rich major contributor to a presidential campaign who can't even speak the language of the country in which he serves, and who knows even less about our own country and our consciousness and our ideals and our motivation, it's an insult to me and to the people of America and to the people of that country."

As former senator and presidential candidate Eugene McCarthy remarked, however, "Certainly it would be an insult, if true. But a check on the eleven countries included in the trip on which Carter supposedly based these comments found that there was no ambassador who was bloated or ignorant . . ., that all but three of the eleven were career diplomats, rather than political appointees, two could speak the language of the country, and the third was learning it."

But that was Candidate Carter, continually conjuring up ogres of obvious amorality—only to chop their heads off, promising, not surprisingly, something different. But what he usually promised was something that "accurately represents the character and the ideals of the American people," "a standard of ethics and morality" that "we have in our own private lives as individuals." Why not?

About four months after his Louisville speech, Carter met three reporters on national television who tried to probe beyond the disingenuous hyperbole.

Syndicated columnist Robert Novak got right to the point. He said that on the campaign trail Carter had always condemned our corpulent and ignorant ambassadors in the context of his foreign policy criticisms and always received a great deal of applause for it.

"Governor," said Novak, "can you name one such fat, ignorant, bloated ambassador who can't speak the language?" It seemed like an obvious enough question.

"No," replied the governor, "I wouldn't want to name any."

Could Carter at least name just one, persisted Novak. "You make the accusation all over. There are only four ambassadors, Governor, who gave contributions to Mr. Nixon. Do any of them fit that category?"

"Well, I wouldn't want to name names," said Carter, the candidate of love and compassion, "but the point that I'm making is . . ."

He was interrupted briefly; but soon got back on his track. "When I've been in foreign countries, and go into embassies, it's obvious from talking to the people in the countries, and talking to the ambassadors, that they are not qualified to be diplomats for this country. They are all [all?] appointed as a political payoff. The point I make is that whether they are actually fat or thin, they are appointed because they are (sic) political interrelationships and not because of quality. Now, the last time I was in Europe, for instance, out of thirty-three ambassadors who served in the whole European theatre, only three of them were professional diplomats. The others were appointed for political reasons."

This was Jimmy Carter at his wiliest—as the verbal gymnast. He wouldn't stoop so low as to defame a man's character by naming.him on national television: everything he said was, quite simply, "obvious."

Novak was fast losing the battle. Almost in desperation he asked if Carter wasn't being demagogic in his "flat statement" about the "fat, bloated, ignorant ambassadors." And the governor responded, "I don't believe so. I think it illustrates a point very clearly." (In fact, the point was that his illustrations were a grotesque caricature paraded about as evidence.)

Finally, Novak, unable to pin the candidate down, asked if he would continue to "use that formulation and get applause from it."

"I may," said Carter characteristically, "or may not."

Carter had won a minor battle in much the same way he won the war: coolly stalking the moral high ground ("I wouldn't want to name names") to avoid admitting that his rhetoric was fallacious; retaking the offensive with an even bolder assertion—again couched in his sanctimonious, above-the-fray phrase, "It's obvious"—that they were "not qualified . . . they are all appointed as political payoffs," a permissible statement because he deigned not to get embroiled in any messy detail; finally manipulating the one "fact" he did have (thirty of thirty-three ambassadors in Europe were not professional diplomats) in such a way as to suggest that it proved that no one was qualified. The candidate had dexterously traveled—in a few short sentences—from the hyperbolic to the ridiculous; from bloated, ignorant, rich and unqualified (and always namelss and undefined) ambassadors to a few people who were not part of the diplomatic corps; from fantasy to trivia.

It was a masterful use of innuendo to suggest an evil whose existence Carter refused to prove. Carter proved himself something of a Don Quixote in the robes of St. George.

Assuming, however, that at least Carter himself believed what he said, he quickly made a mockery of his words upon assuming the presidency. His ambassadorial appointments list read as if it were taken from the who's who of political patronage. And quite a few of President Carter's emissaries would not be found among the ranks of "professional diplomats."

To Brussels went Anne Cox Chambers, Atlanta newspaper heiress and an early and enthusiastic contributor to the campaigns of Jimmy Carter. The American Foreign Service Association, an elite group of former professional diplomats, tagged the appointment a political payoff.

The Australians were to welcome Philip Henry Alston, whose foreign service credentials were summed up neatly in the latest edition of *Who's Who in American Politics:* "US Ambassador to Australia, Dept. of State, 77-" That was all. He was kind of an on-the-job trainee. His credentials for service in the administration of Jimmy Carter were far more impressive: rich lawyer; contributor to the Carter election campaign; head of the Atlanta law firm which represented Bert Lance and supplied the Carter camp with its "ethics" adviser; member of the advisory board of Citizens and Southern National Bank which had loaned money to Carter; and a director of a number of corporations.

Leonard Woodcock had signed on with the Carter team for the Florida primary and endorsed the Georgian in May of 1976. His support meant more than dollars for Carter: Woodcock happened to be president of one of the most politically potent trade-unions in the country, the United Automobile Workers. His reward, despite the fact that he had no foreign diplomatic experience, was an appointment to head the U.S. Liaison Office in Peking.

How many other "professional diplomats" did Carter send off to foreign lands? Here are a few who were not drawn from the foreign service ranks:

Ulric St. Clair Haynes Jr., vice-president of Cummins Engine Company, to Algeria.

Philip M. Kaiser, director of Guiness Mahon Holdings Ltd. (a British bank holding company) to Hungary.

Louis A. Lerner, publisher of Lerner Newspapers in Chicago, to Norway.

Patrick Lucey, Democratic governor of Wisconsin, to Mexico.

William V. Shannon, New York *Times* editorial board, to Ireland.

Mabel Murphy Smythe, vice-president of the Phelps-Stokes Fund, to the Republic of Cameroon.

Marvin L. Warner, chairman of the Warner National Corporation, to Switzerland.

John C. West, lawyer and former governor of South Carolina, to Saudi Arabia.

Milton A. Wolf, construction company president in Cleveland, to Austria.

Were these men and women "qualified" to represent the United States in foreign lands? By Candidate Carter's standards, no.

Jimmy Carter seemed not so much a man for all seasons as for all reasons. He was not so much the politician on stage as he was a revolving mannequin in a storefront window, pretending to be exposed to the passers-by who gawked at his revolutions but were really enthralled by their own reflection in the glass. The fascination with Carter seemed oddly removed from the normal judgments made about candidates. He was indeed an enigma. But the real puzzle about Jimmy Carter was with what dexterity he managed to convince so many people that his potential lay somehow buried beneath the enigma, the contradiction, the inconsistency, the willful deceptions and fabrications—the more inchoate, the greater the potential.

Some Carter watchers were drawn to the candidate's contradictions as were petitioners to the Delphi oracle— often for reasons not altogether very profound or even relevent to a presidential election. "I see no middle ground for him," wrote Stanley Cloud of *Time* in his magazine's glowing Jimmy Carter-Man-of-the-Year Award issue after the election, "no mediocrity. He often described his vision of America as a 'beautiful mosaic' of almost infinite colors and facets." That may have been fine for a poet, but what was significant about that for Cloud was that "Presidents don't normally talk that way. They don't normally cry in front of reporters. They don't normally blast some political opponent one day and apologize publicly the next." All of this may have been reason for a modest degree of empathy for Carter, but it hardly merited the kind of mystical storm which Cloud showered upon it. "Presidents don't normally do a lot of things Jimmy Carter does. Therein

lies his mystery. Therein lies his potential for greatness—
or the possibility of disaster."

David Broder of the Washington *Post* described a typical
Carter campaign technique where the candidate told a
black audience that he would "never deliberately mislead
you," "school integration, I'm for it"; and in front of a
white audience the same day "Forced busing, I don't like
it." Carter, thought Broder, left many people wondering
whether to hail him as "the most promising political figure
to emerge in the 1970's" or dismiss him outright as "the
most skillful demagogue."

In fact, the combination of the hot and cold Carter, the
blasting and apologetic, the promising politician and the
skillful demagogue were better forebodings of a tepid
president than either a great or disastrous one.

As a campaigner Carter was a fundamentalist. He knew
his audience; he was at his best in small gatherings, kissing
babies, hugging little old ladies, listening intently; he sent
his pollster out to measure the winds of public opinion; he
slept in the homes of his supporters because he wanted to
know how they felt; he condemned what was their evil,
promised what was their good. Neither he nor any other
candidate would determine the issues: the issues "exist in
the minds and hearts of our citizens."

Calling ambassadors "bloated," "ignorant" and "rich"
was not demagogic for him because that was what the electorate expected him to say. "Strangely," observed Eugene
McCarthy, "this is not the demagoguery of America
against which we were warned by Tocqueville nearly one
hundred fifty years ago. It is not classical, detached,
Machiavellian demagoguery. It is inherent, personal, almost natural."

Carter was not a trickster or exploiter or demagogue in
spite of himself, but because of himself. He wanted to be
liked by the voters, by people, by all those folks with whom

he had or wanted a personal, intimate relationship. The issues were like so many disparate, fleeting, unattached and impersonal lumps of clay to be molded and used, always subservient to the dictates of the people. To the degree that the people loved an issue, so would Jimmy Carter support it, because he loved the people, each and every one.

He wasn't concerned that he be remembered in the history books for any great social program, any particular vision of American society that would define and enlighten a few important proposals for change. "It's too hard to know now," he said only a few months before assuming the presidential mantle, "what I'd single out as programs to be remembered by." There seemed to be very little beyond his "hope" that "people will say, 'You know, Jimmy Carter made a lot of mistakes, but he never told a lie.' " But that was not so much a noble ideal as a simple bottom line. He had no program priorities beyond "the generic concern" that would "guide me in all the decisions I make—on welfare, taxes, transportation, energy, on the regulatory agencies"—and that was "the desire to let the people have a sense it's their government and to make that government, newly reorganized, a source of inspiration."

What Carter was describing seemed more a program for a nationwide sensitivity session than constructive and creative reform. His highest priorities were communications of feelings—to abolish secrecy, to create openness, to be honest and loving and compassionate; to give the people "a sense" of their government. "Every time we've made a serious mistake in recent years in our dealing with other nations, the American people have been excluded from the process of evolving and consummating foreign policy. *Indeed the mistakes have been because of the secrecy.* (Emphasis added.) There was nothing ignoble about advocating an open government, but Carter seemed to equate secrecy with substance, the covering-up and the *what* of the cover-up.

It was a subtle confusion usually jumbled by familiar Carter buzz words. In a short soliloquy for *Playboy* he said that "Our government should justify the character and moral principles of the American people, and our foreign policy should not short-circuit that for temporary advantage. I think in every instance we've done that it's been counterproductive. When the CIA undertakes covert activities that might be justified if they were peaceful, we always suffer when they're revealed. . . ."

In three consecutive sentences he moved without transition from the advocacy of "moral principles"; to warning of "counterproductive" (i.e., a principle of, if anything, pragmatism, not morality) results; immediately to the dangers (suffering) of "revealed" CIA activities. Were those three ideas linked by anything more than proximity? Was Carter suggesting that justifying moral principles meant acting in a way that was not counterproductive, and that not being counterproductive meant not revealing CIA activities? Was that his moral principle? Did he think that the honesty and decency and compassion in the character of the American people demanded an aversion to the mentality that the exposés revealed or simply and simplistically an avoidance of the exposés themselves? Some people believed he meant the former; others, the latter. Carter himself, somehow believed in both: he began by implying that he wanted to change ships of state, and ended by saying he would be satisfied in staying aboard and simply swabbing the deck. He obviously couldn't do both, but he didn't seem to realize it.

Carter seemed to confuse the goals of government with the process of governing. What his foreign *policy* would be, what domestic policies would be stressed, what the substance of government activity would be, what would be communicated beyond the desire to communicate—these concerns were subsumed by his two unenlightening and constantly repeated procedural goals of openness and competence. There would be a great, honest outpouring of feelings and hopes that, however contradictory and confused, would relieve the guilt and solve the nation's problems. If Tom Wolfe called this "the ME Decade," Jimmy Carter would be its civil manifestation, leading the country in a grand surge of national narcissism.

Carter himself shed some light on his peculiar approach to the art of politicking and governing in recounting two different incidences from his non-political past. The first was a brief encounter with a Baptist minister with whom he "had one of the most moving religious experience of my life." The second was a seemingly innocent meeting with his mother which Carter "vividly" remembered.

In the late 1960s, as part of the Southern Baptist Crusades to the north, Carter journeyed to Springfield, Massachussetts, to work in a ghetto of predominantly Spanish-speaking families. His guide and co-worker, as Carter explains in *Why Not The Best?*, was a Cuban-born minister named Eloy Cruz, who Carter thought was "one of the best men I have ever know." For "an inspiring week" the two worked together, visiting the poor and underprivileged, offering their counsel and prayer. Carter's description of the week barely spans two pages of his book, even though during a visit with a dejected young man Carter said he "had one of the most moving religious experiences of my life" (about which he said no more, however). But the most important thing learned from Cruz, and Carter takes the title for the entire chapter from the minister's admonition, was, "You only need to have two loves: one for God, and one for the person standing in front of you at any given moment."

Carter's fond memory of Cruz and his commandment is

interesting because it seems to explain something about the perils of applying religious precepts to the political process. If nothing more, a love "for the person standing in front of you at any given moment" became a partial metaphor for the peculiar kind of "demagogic" campaign and frustrated presidency that Carter brought to the seventies. Candidate Carter would stand in front of blacks, saying he was for integration; and in front of whites, he was against forced busing. For Catholics, he was against abortion; for the rest, he said he didn't favor a constitutional amendment which would ban it. He told black audiences that Martin Luther King, Jr., was a great American hero; he didn't mention King to the whites. It was not the skill of a demagogue which led Carter into such seemingly deceptive campaign tactics as much as it was the zeal of a man who believed he could be all things to all men.

When Carter was asked on television—with the nation as audience—whether his omission of King was intentional, he said, not surprisingly, no, it wasn't. But, he explained, "I always intentionally put Martin Luther King's name in if there were black people in the audience, because he was a great American."

Why then leave it out in front of the whites? "Well, it was not a deliberate thing, and it won't be done anymore, but it was just a reaction to the audience, and the leaders in which they would be interested."

On its face, Carter's explanation made little sense. How could he "intentionally" add a name to a list without at the same time "deliberately" omitting it? If he were intent on not forgetting King's name, why was he not conscious of omitting it? There was no logical explanation except that from the shrewd politician: the list was not, after all, one of great Americans, it was a list of "leaders in which they (i.e., the audience standing directly in front of him) would be interested." There was nothing deliberate, intentional, conscious or even rational about the whole thing, "it was just a reaction to the audience."

In another brief flash on the past Carter tells the readers of *Why Not The Best* about a moment of indecision from his childhood that seemed to be of some significance to him. He was a normal kid, he says, and "like all farm boys" he always carried his trusty slingshot around with him and always had a few pebbles in his pocket for ammunition. Not just any old pebbles: they were "little white round rocks,"; "the most perfectly shaped rocks of proper size," ones that he only found along the Seaboard Railroad track. He even had his little caches of pebble hidden around the farm just in case "I ran out of my pocket supply."

"One day," wrote the former governor, "I was leaving the track with my pockets full of rocks, and my mother came out on the front porch and called me. She had in her hands a plate full of cookies which she had just baked for me. She asked, 'Honey, would you like some cookies?' Really, nothing much happened, but I still remember it vividly. I stood there about fifteen or twenty seconds, in honest doubt about whether I should drop those worthless rocks and take the cookies which Mother offered me with a heart full of love."

There Carter ends the narration, leaving his readers curiously in suspense about whether he did or did not drop the pebbles, except for the hint in the next paragraph: "It is hard to understand why we were so reluctant to drop the rocks of past years." What was curious about Carter's recollection of this incident was not his moral lesson about giving up the "rocks of past years," but rather how quickly his "little white round rocks" of "perfect shape" and "proper size" became "worthless." And it wasn't even that the stones were suddenly made worthless because of a plate full of mouthwatering cookies (they were just "the cookies"), but rather because "Mother offered [them to] me with a heart full of love." For Carter (at least for the Jimmy Carter who remembered the event so many years later) it was not a question of exchanging rocks for cookies, but of giving up something of personal value so as not to forfeit the love of his mother. And perhaps Carter was so vague about whether he actually dropped the pebbles (a vagueness even more curious because his stated reason for bringing the whole incident up was to teach a lesson about the value of dropping them) because he wasn't really sure he had made the right decision after all: giving up something of value in return for motherly love.

During the campaign for the presidency, Carter was always faced with the dilemma of explaining past actions that in retrospect were seen as weak and conciliatory by his critics: the abdication of principle for popularity or simply lack of concern.

He was a hawk on Vietnam until the "general feeling" and his status as a "public official" made it safe at least to say that the war was not winnable.

In 1971, immediately after Lt. William Calley had been convicted of the My Lai massacres by an Army tribunal in Georgia, Governor Carter declared American Serviceman's Day and advised all motorists to drive with their lights on. The critics in 1976 immediately brought him to the mat for his apparent disregard for the value of human life in what seemed to be open support of Calley's action.

But as Carter the candidate for president explained it, "I don't think that was said in support of or in opposition to the conviction of Lt. Calley." (Did he or did he not drop the stones?) ". . . it was a very highly emotional thing; and rather than focusing the attention of Georgia people on the Calley case itself, I tried to hold down violence and to take the sharp edge off the Calley conviction . . . by saying let's think about all of our fighting men who did perform well." If Carter did not support Calley, neither did he condemn him (until much later). At the crucial moment of decision, he followed the path of least resistance; he opted to take the "sharp edge" off "a very emotional thing." And by proclamation, Carter declared the slaughter of innocent women and children a non-issue.

Carter was proud of the fact that when he was a struggling entrepreneur in Plains during the fifties, he had risked his financial future and his physical well-being by standing up to the town's bully segregationists. Most of the other whites in Plains joined the White Citizens Council; but when the chief of police and the railroad depot agent (also a Baptist preacher) visited Carter's peanut warehouse to inform him that every other white male adult in town had joined and that it wouldn't look good (his customers would quit coming around and the chief wouldn't guarantee his safety) if he didn't go along, Carter refused. "My response was that I had no intention of joining the organization on any basis; that I was willing to leave Plains if necessary; that the five dollars dues requirement was not an important factor; and that I would never change my mind."

This incident and others—like his unveiling of Martin Luther King's portrait in the state capitol, his appointment of blacks to governmental posts in his gubernatorial administration—were marched before the national electorate in 1976 as signs of Carter's truly enlightened and liberal attitude toward civil rights.

Skeptics, however, were also finding evidence to suggest that Carter was a closet racist. He embraced Lester Maddox and White Citizens Council organizer Roy Harris in his 1970 gubernatorial campaign. He became embroiled in a campaign broohaha in the closing moments of his race against Gerald Ford because he told a reporter that he favored maintaining the "ethnic purity" of neighborhoods; he was a member of an avowed segregated church; he was against forced busing.

The pros and cons seemed to suggest nothing more than Carter was no more racist than he was flaming integrationist. Civil rights had never been Jimmy Carter's concern until it had first become the main concern of the public. He was hailed in *Time* magazine after his gubernatorial election for his ringing pledge, "I say to you quite frankly that the time for racial discrimination is over," but his kudos were that the words "heralded the end" of an era. As Carter said in the same innaugural speech, "Our people have already made this major and difficult decision."

Carter was not risking his livelihood because of a civil rights principle when he snubbed the White Citizens Council in the fifties. He was protecting his reputation as leading citizen of Plains; a man whose family had weather-beaten and craggy roots sunk deep in the dusty back-woods south Georgia land, deeper than those of any police chief or railroad agent. His father had farmed thousands of acres, sweated a lot, and treated his black workers with the kindly diffidence of a patrician landlord; the Carter's were the first family of Plains; Jimmy was the brightest kid in town, he worked hard, he went to Annapolis, became an officer in the Navy, saw the world (or at least some of it), met senators and admirals and was on his way to becoming Chief of Naval Operations for the entire United States Navy. He had outgrown Plains, was finding his success in a much larger world. Then suddenly his father died, and he gave it all up; dropped his fistful of pebbles and went back to Plains to save the family business. If he had renounced all that—his carefully guarded and nurtured dream of the Navy career—for the sake of his family and his roots (not for his wife Rosalynn, however, who "disagreed violently" and feared that "our married freedom might be cramped or partially dominated by relatives, particularly his mother and my mother"). No penny-ante policeman or railroad agent or all the citizens of Plains would force anything down his throat. Race was only a superficial issue. The real issue was Jimmy Carter.

And so it remained: As Carter wooed support for governor by exploiting racial biases, as he unveiled portraits of Martin Luther King, as he continued to attend a segregated church, as he promised blacks in 1976 that he would "rather die" than lose the confidence they had in him.

Carter had set himself up perfectly for the buffeting he was to receive in the presidency. In the overreaching drive to reassure the electorate that he was a man of the people, whose "strength" was his "personal relationship" with them, he offered little idea of what, if any, unifying vision would set his priorities. He pulled into the Oval Office a long string of promises which offered more of everything for everybody, but no serious commitment to anything in particular.

There was cause for disillusionment from the very beginning. Suddenly, upon taking office, there was a great deal of confusion about what kind of an outsider Jimmy Carter really was. "I owe special interests nothing. I owe the people everything. And I'm going to keep it that way," he had promised. But like so much else that Carter said about himself, there was plenty of ground to doubt the premise, and good reason to question the promise.

"We have been governed too long by people who are isolated from the realities of life in America," Candidate Carter told the National Conference of Catholic Charities in Denver. "Our leaders have spent too many years strolling down the plush green fairways of privilege. They seem not to know that there is hunger and despair in America."

Someone in the Carter administration would probably

be able to explain what their populist *really* meant when he uttered those words, but somehow no amount of Carter exegesis could explain away the many new appointees who were no strangers either to the plush green fairways of privilege or Washington power.

Hamilton Jordan had made the mistake of getting specific about who was who on the insider list in the least prescient of all campaign remarks: "If, after the inauguration, you find a Cy Vance as Secretary of State and Zbigniew Brzezinski as head of National Security, then I would say we failed. And I'd quit. But that's not going to happen. You're going to see new faces, new ideas. The government is going to be run by people you have never heard of before."

Jordan was wrong on every score but the "we failed" part (though he changed his mind about them after the election—of Vance, he remarked, "He runs the State Department as well as it can be run."). And his boss began looking sillier with each announcement of a new "outsider" joining the administration. No matter what Jimmy Carter was running *against* in 1976—be it Washington, or privilege, or big shots, or secrecy, or the status quo, or the powerful, or the influential, et cetera—his administration was *it* in 1977. Whether a lie, or a deception, or broken promise, the new roster of the most powerful men in Washington represented the first of many insults heaped on the people by the born-again candidate, who railed about the "major and fundamental issue taking shape in this election year. That issue is the division between the 'insiders' and the 'outsiders.' . . . The people of this country know from bitter experience that we are not going to get these changes merely by shifting around the same group of insiders. . . . The insiders have had their chance and they have not delivered. And their time has run out. The time has come for the great majority of Americans—

those who have for too long been on the outside looking in—to have a president who will turn the government of this country inside out."

How did the new president go about turning the government inside out? He didn't. Reaching into his bag of tricks, Carter managed to accomplish the not-very-difficult task of choosing a government of men and women who had spent most of their adult lives traipsing about the fairways of privilege and the corridors of power.

As Secretary of State he chose a man who thought that Henry Kissinger was "a genius, no doubt about it." Cyrus Vance had a reputation for "leaving no footprints" in his decade and a half march on the insiders treadmill. After an ivy-league education at Yale, Vance joined a prestigious Manhattan law firm which served as training ground for his entry into government with the Kennedy administration. From 1960 to 1967 Vance served in key positions of the war establishment: General Counsel to the Defense Department, Secretary of the Army, and Deputy Secretary of Defense. He was finally a Special Assistant to Lyndon Johnson before retiring again to New York, there to wait out the Nixon years as a successful corporate lawyer and director of the Rockefeller Foundation, Pan Am, IBM and the New York *Times.* Even before Jimmy Carter began warming the ears of the outsiders with his promises, the insiders, who knew how the old adage about *plus ca change, plus c'est le meme chose* applied to government, were making their predictions. David Scheiderman, an assistant editor of the Op-Ed page of the New York *Times* related in an April 1976 issue of *Harper's* an interesting exchange he had with a "top-ranking official" of the Council on Foreign Relations, the "New York City clubhouse" of the foreign policy Establishment:

"Who is the number one candidate for Secretary of State?"

"Cy Vance."

"Why?"

"If the Establishment chairman is John McCloy [former chairman of Chase Manhattan bank *inter alia*], and David Rockefeller [chairman of Chase *inter alia*] is president, then Cy Vance is vice-president. This is the line of succession."

"Nobody has anything against him. Find me a man who doesn't like Cy Vance. Vance is the man everyone respects. He's brilliant at having everyone admire him. Cy Vance has got to be Secretary of State or there's something wrong with this country."

Candidate Carter was either naive or devious with his diagnoses about what was wrong with the country: his rhetoric suggested, as his assistants overtly stated, that men like Cy Vance were *exactly* what was wrong. But, the beat went on.

To fill the job of Secretary of Defense, Carter chose a man who once suggested (in his capacity as Secretary of the Air Force) the bombing of the civilian population of North Vietnam while directing Lyndon Johnson's bombing of the rest of the country. Harold Brown was something of a child prodigy in nuclear physics, earning a Ph.D. from Columbia in the field before taking his genius for numbers, science, and administration to the Defense Department during both the Kennedy and Johnson regimes. There, under the tutelage of the man who loved charting the continuous destruction of Vietnam with pretty graphs and charts, Robert McNamara, Brown rose quickly in the military establishment, eventually landing his job as head of the Air Force. He left Washington in 1969 to acquire the presidency of the California Institute of Technology, bringing the school lucrative government contracts, while working part-time for the Republicans on the SALT delegation and sitting on the boards of several companies, including IBM, with Vance.

There was one interesting coincidence and a curious

irony connecting Brown and Jimmy Carter. While Secretary of the Air Force, Brown had been exceedingly embarrassed by a Pentagon employee who testified before Congress about a two billion dollar cost overrun on the C-5A transport; and he quickly ran the truthful tattler, Ernest Fitzgerald, out of the Pentagon. The case was made-to-order for Candidate Carter who used it to remind the electorate once again what kind of president he would be: "The Fitzgerald case," said Carter in the closing moments of the campaign, "where a dedicated civil servant was fired from the Defense Department for reporting cost overruns, must never be repeated." The coincidence, of course, was naming Fitzgerald's former boss and nemesis as head of the Pentagon. The irony was that Jimmy Carter's Justice Department opposed Fitzgerald in his suit to gain reinstatement to his old job at the Pentagon.

The reins of Health, Education and Welfare, the bureaucratic giant which dispersed more than a third of the entire federal budget toward the maintenance of the social fabric, were inherited by a corporate lawyer who had earned more than five hundred thousand dollars in 1976. Joseph Califano, like Vance and Brown, had worked at McNamara's Defense Department, and was put on a special project after the 1967 Detroit riot to monitor potential domestic hot spots (a venture that turned out to be a mini-scale CIA type covert operation). It was Califano who recommended Alexander Haig, an underling of his at Defense, to Henry Kissinger in 1969; and it was Haig who went on to stand next to Richard Nixon as his loyal chief of staff during the final year, and then on to be NATO Supreme Commander, his position during the Carter administration. As a law partner of Edward Bennett Williams during the Nixon years, Califano remained in Washington to reap lucrative rewards from counseling such large companies as Coca-Cola.

Most of the other top appointments to the Carter administration were equally noted for their long service
either to the Washington bureaucracy or the corporate
establishment or, in most cases, to both.

The Secretary of Housing and Urban Development,
Patricia Harris, boasted twenty-nine honorary degrees and
forty memberships on the boards of such companies as
Chase Manhattan, IBM, Scott Paper, and the National
Bank of Washington. She had been Johnson's ambassador
to Luxembourg.

Juanita Kreps, Secretary of Commerce, was a member
of the board of eight different companies, including such
establishment power houses as R. J. Reynolds tobacco, the
New York Stock Exchange, and Eastman Kodak, while
serving as a vice-president of Duke University and lecturer
at the University of North Carolina.

And if there were some myth about anyone from Georgia being, by definition, an outsider, the biographies of
Budget Director and national banktrotter Bert Lance and
Attorney General Griffin Bell served as reminders that a
southern accent is no bar to the plush paths of privilege.
Appointed to the federal circuit judgeship in Atlanta in
1960 by Kennedy after running his Georgian presidential
campaign, Bell by 1977 was earning a yearly income (he
quit the court in the spring of 1976) of some one hundred
fifty thousand dollars, a result, in part, of his partnership
in Atlanta's most prestigious law firm (the same one, King
and Spalding, of which Carter confidant Charles Kirbo
was a partner) and investments in Coca-Cola (also his legal
client as it was Califano's) and the National Bank of Georgia (remember Bert Lance).

A part of Bell's problems at his Senate confirmation
hearings stemmed from a spotty record as judge, but more
critically, a less-than-admirable reputation (some critics
hinted at racism) on civil rights issues. His membership in

the two most important "social" clubs of Atlanta—the Capital City and the Piedmont Driving Club—both noted for their not-quite-official closed-door policy on Jews and blacks; his court decision to uphold the prevention of black state representative-elect Julian Bond from taking his seat in the Georgia legislature because he'd opposed the Vietnam war and the draft (later unanimously overturned by the Supreme Court); and his service during the fifties as chief of staff to Governor Ernest Vandiver (who once said, "I make this solemn pledge to the mothers and fathers and to the people: when Ernest Vandiver is your governor, neither my three children, nor any of yours, will ever attend a racially mixed school or college in this state") did little to promote confidence in Jimmy Carter's claim to shake the government up—let alone turn it inside out.

According to Roger Morris, a former member of the National Security Council and various Senate staffs, the eleven "outsiders" on Jimmy Carter's cabinet had some seventy cumulative years on the public payroll, some thirty corporate directorships and an average 1976 income of two hundred eleven thousand dollars. "Ironically," said Morris, "what most distinguishes Jimmy Carter's 'outsiders' from that [Nixon] GOP regime of privilege and power is that present cabinet members are individually and collectively far wealthier."

If there was little difference between the pedigrees of the Nixon appointees and those of Carter, the biggest difference between Nixon as an establishment politician and Carter in the same garb was that the former's ties to a power elite were taken for granted while the latter's spawned conspiracy theories.

Carter spent nearly two years drawing around him thousands of supporters who believed his criticisms of the status quo and the incestuous relationship between the big shots of business, law, finance, and government; and thought that Jimmy Carter heralded a change in the winds of power-brokering in Washington. Instead, he tapped the same sources as his predecessors and, not surprisingly, wound up with familiar faces.

Mr. Vance, Mr. Brown, and Mrs. Harris were all on IBM board of directors. In Atlanta the giant computer company was represented by King and Spalding, Griffin Bell's law firm, and in Los Angeles by the firm of Carter's appointee as Deputy Secretary of State, Warren M. Christopher. The Secretary of the Army, Clifford Alexander, was a partner in a large Washington law firm; as was Carter's new Secretary of the Navy, W. Graham Clayton. Clayton also had served as a president and director of the Southern Railway Company, a director of J. P. Morgan and Company, and a director of the Morgan Guaranty Trust Company.

Both Carter's national security affairs adviser, Zbigniew Brzezinski, and his czar of energy, James Schlesinger (later Secretary of Energy), were associates at the Rand Corporation. His Deputy Secretary of the Treasury, Kenneth S. Axelson, was a senior executive at J. C. Penney, one of whose board members was Juanita Kreps, the new Commerce Secretary.

Charles Duncan, the Deputy Secretary of Defense, was a former president of Coca-Cola, another client of Bell's firm in Atlanta and Joseph Califano's in Washington.

Carter named Clark Clifford, a Secretary of Defense for Lyndon Johnson, as his special envoy to Cyprus (Clifford was later called in as a lawyer for Bert Lance). He appointed Elliot L. Richardson, a Republican who had served in four cabinet posts and as an ambassador to Britain in the previous eight years, his ambassador at large. And he called on an Assistant Secretary of Defense under Johnson, Paul Warnke, to be his chief disarmament negotiator.

"The thing that's really absolutely remarkable," David Cohen, president of the public affairs lobby Common Cause, told James Wooten, "is that, whether the president's from Georgia or Massachusetts, it's the same university axis that's dominant." He might have added, the same corporate, financial, legal, and bureaucratic axis as well.

And, as Wooten concluded, "the circle seems unbroken. After Secretaries Brown, Vance and Harris resigned from their jobs as directors of IBM, the corporation announced that two of the vacancies had been filled. "The new directors are William W. Scranton, who recently left his job as the United States representative to the United Nations, and William T. Coleman, Jr., who was President Ford's Secretary of Transportation."

For the rest, there was more of the same. Besides the missed opportunities at the cabinet level, Carter botched a chance to fill positions at twenty-five key regulatory agencies and effect some significant change—or even tip the balance—by dredging the same tired waters. "For all of Jimmy Carter's rhetoric about new faces," said Paul Sturm of *Forbes* magazine about the regulatory agency jobs, "there are few of them and the selection process hasn't changed since Harry Truman."

Of those twenty-five appointees all but four came from the traditional breeding ground for regulatory agency heads—academic institutions or the government—and many were political payoffs. In some cases the results were abysmally monotonous: the new chief at the Federal Maritime Commission came from the Senate Commerce Committee; the new chief at the Interstate Commerce Commission came from the Senate Commerce Committee; the new chief at the Federal Trade Commission came from the Senate Commerce Committee. There were two field directors of the 1976 Carter campaign and a former deputy chairman of the Democratic National Committee who moved into forty-seven-thousand-five-hundred-dollar-a-year slots on the Copyright Royalty Tribunal; and there was an Indianapolis banker who directed Carter's Indiana campaign ("Regulatory agencies," said Carter as a campaigner, "must not be managed by representatives of the industry being regulated.") to take over at the Federal Home Loan Bank Board.

To make the incestuous monotony complete, James King, the man who directed the Carter White House personnel office, wound up—at fifty-two thousand five hundred dollars a year—as head of the National Transportation Safety Board.

Carter was able to turn his lack of notoriety into the catch-all sobriquet "outsider," eventually a trademark that seemed to stand for almost anything that Jimmy Carter was or was said to be. *Time* magazine, in its long summation of the marathon campaign, unhesitatingly called him "the typical outsider." Carter "demolished all the axioms" with his "flinty will power." For *Time,* and perhaps for much of the nation, more than ten million of whom read its consistently glowing reports, that meant that Carter was "a rather different politician . . . different in philosophy and tactics . . . in personal style . . . he is still an enigma. . . . complex . . . contradictory . . . people did not even know who he was. He occupied no political office." The irony was that *Time* should have known who Carter was. Almost seven years before, it had dedicated its first cover to him, saying some of the same things, calling Carter "both product and destroyer of old myths. . . . looking eerily like John Kennedy . . ., Carter is a man as contradictory as Georgia itself. . . ."

One of the interesting differences, however between the *Time* account of 1971 and that of 1977—and there were remarkably very few—was the rewriting of history that seemed to come from the need for a new Carter fable, one that would fit the mantle of a president.

In 1971, for example, Governor Carter's ancestors had

been "in southwest Georgia for one hundred fifty years—cotton farmers, Civil War soldiers, merchants and businessmen." But by 1977, President Carter "stem(med) from two hundred forty years of Southern yeomanry whose natural enemies were bankers and big landlords." It seemed to be a required change: In 1971 Carter had to be a symbol of the New South, growing and changing toward an "urbanized and industrialized" modern society like the rest of the country; but in 1977, Carter was the renegade whose "heart belongs to the vibrant populism that he acquired—as naturally as his accent—while growing up on a South Georgia farm during the Depression." In 1971, Carter's populism seemed much more pragmatic, by *Time*'s account: Carter simply "appealed to the ever-potent populist instincts" of the electorate.

Time of 1971 said that Jimmy Carter, "during his election for state senator (1962) . . . found some irregularities in one of the ballot boxes" and "the election was reversed in his favor."

By 1977 the event was seen somewhat more romantically as the underdog's (read *outsider*) triumph over the establishment: "Carter's tenacity is extraordinary. Apparently defeated in his first try for the state senate . . ., he fought to prove ballot stuffing by the boss of Quitman County. . . . Governor-elect Carl Sanders, among other officials, was indifferent to Carter's righteous demands, thus fanning his suspicion of the 'vested interests.' "

1971: Carter "beat former Governor Carl Sanders in the Democratic runoff and went on to a 200,000-vote victory over the Republican candidate. . . ."

1977: ". . . and settling another personal score, [Carter] defeated Sanders for the governorship in 1970 after a particularly bitter campaign."

In 1971 Carter's business acumen and wealth seemed to be important to the story, *Time* announcing that Carter

Warehouses was grossing eight hundred thousand dollars annually and his family owned two thousand five hundred acres of land.

In 1977, *Time* relegated Carter's wealth to a footnote, even though his business in 1975 grossed 2.5 million dollars and his personal wealth was nearly nine hundred thousand dollars.

As it turned out, he was just as much a beneficiary of the "insiders" system as was his friend Bert Lance or his associate David Rockefeller.

Carter played dexterously on the myth that the defining attribute of the American ruling class was geography— hence, the codeword "outsider," the symbolic importance of Plains, Georgia, and the equally important decision to keep his campaign headquarters in Atlanta. As long as he maintained the physical distance from New York and Washington, he could enjoy more advantages from his outsider image than the metaphor really implied—anti-big shot, anti-establishment, anti-Washington, a man for the people, the folks out there. But there was more to being an outsider than simply coming from Plains, Georgia.

As was the case with the chieftains who pow-wowed at the Council on Foreign Relations over who was going to inherit the domain at the State Department, other members of the establishment knew their Jimmy Carter—long before the people did.

In the closing days of 1972, while Carter and his close advisers in Atlanta were secretly devising strategy for an assault on the White House, Milton Katz, the director of International Legal Studies at Harvard and a board member of the Carnegie Endowment for International Peace, received a strange call from the ageless major domo of Washington politics, Averell Harriman.

"We've got to get off our high horses," said Harriman to

Katz at one point, "and look at some of these southern governors."

Harriman then mentioned three of them; and Jimmy Carter was at the head of the class.

Ironically, a couple of years later, in the spring of 1974 and still months before Carter announced his candidacy, Katz received a letter from the Georgia governor asking for a campaign contribution. Katz later joined the Carter camp, as did Harriman. The latter, the confidant of five different presidents, was eventually enlisted as a Carter foreign policy adviser before the election and at one point even visited Moscow to, as the New York *Times* reported, "calm Soviet fears about the effect of election-year speeches on detente."

The fears of the east coast establishment about the possibility of a renegade outsider usurping its power had apparently been calmed years before Carter's 1976 rhetorical blitzkrieg, as Harriman's call to Katz suggested. He had, in a number of ways proved his allegiance to the values shared by the ruling class before Harriman's call and many years before he rewarded its standard-bearers by turning his federal government over to them.

A minor incident almost a decade before was illustrative of the fact that though Carter may have been a small fish in the large pond of national power, he was a fish all the same. There was a time in 1965 when Carter, already a Georgia legislator and successful agribusinessman, had contemplated becoming a banker.

He approached the Small Business Administration and the Citizens' Bank of Americus that year to ask a favor: he wanted to reclaim some two hundred acres of Georgia land that he had used as collateral in negotiating a one hundred seventy-five thousand dollar loan three years earlier. That money had been used to construct and equip an agricultural warehouse and Carter explained that he needed the land free of mortgage so he could borrow more money to expand his business again.

Both the SBA and Citizens' Bank, however, turned him down. Why? Because they suspected that Carter really wanted the money for political and personal reasons.

At the time Carter was considering running for the House of Representatives against Howard Callaway (though after Callaway decided to run for governor instead, Carter changed his mind about Congress and entered the gubernatorial race as well), and both the SBA and the bank believed that he wanted the money for the campaign as well as to start up his own rival bank in Americus.

"Mr. Carter had admitted," said Max Houston, an SBA official in Atlanta, "and the (Citizens') Bank is also aware of it, that the primary reason was to obtain the necessary funds in starting another bank in Americus," and "to enter a political race against Congressman Callaway."

Carter eventually lost his gubernatorial bid in 1966. But he went on to win in 1970, this time with the help of some rather influential Georgians.

During the presidential campaign Carter tried to avoid the details of the contacts which served as an important financial power-base in his successful 1970 race. When asked on national television in the spring of 1976 who his gubernatorial campaign contributors were, Carter responded that because Georgia had no disclosure law at the time "nobody ever made a report of contributors and we didn't maintain those records." (It was a bit odd that the man who was going to make government more efficient and competent didn't even bother to keep tabs on the source of his money; and also quite a bit out of character for the fanatically well organized Jimmy Carter who boasted in his autobiography that after each day of campaigning he would meticulously dictate "names, informa-

tion about the community, and speech notes for later use
. . . into a small tape recorder in the automobile" and the
next day have his wife write "thank-you notes on an automatic typewriter which also recorded names, addresses,
and code descriptions of the persons I had met.")

However, Phil Stanford, a Washington-based journalist,
reported in a summer issue of the *Columbia Journalism Review,* that he "checked with two accountants who worked
for Carter's campaign in 1970 and both told me that the
campaign organization kept records of all contributions.
One of them, Richard Harden, a CPA whom Carter later
appointed to an important position in his administration,
said that the contribution lists were kept by computer, and
that Carter's campaign managers received a monthly
print-out of all contributors." (That sounded more like the
Jimmy Carter from *Why Not The Best?.*)

That kind of evidence—not to mention the fact that it
appeared somewhat hypocritical for the candidate who
was promising openness in all facets of government to hide
behind the technicality of a Georgia non-disclosure law as
reason for not coming clean—finally forced the Carter
camp to release a list of gubernatorial contributors, but not
until October seventeenth, eight months after denying the
list's existence. Some of the names on the list may have
explained why Jimmy "I've never had the support of
powerful special-interest groups" Carter held out for so
long. Fewer than three hundred people accounted for
some three hundred seventy thousand dollars in contributions, half the total amount raised; and corporations alone
gave fifty-seven thousand dollars.

The chairman of the board of Atlanta Newspapers Inc.
and heir to the Cox newspaper fortune, Anne Cox Chambers, and her husband kicked in over thirty thousand dollars. (In 1977 Mrs. Chambers went to Belgium as a United
States ambassador.)

Other contributors were equally prominent in their particular spheres of influence: Philip Alston, head of a prestigious Atlanta law firm (and later Carter's ambassador to Australia); Robert Lipshutz, the Atlanta lawyer who was treasurer of both the gubernatorial and presidential campaigns (and later became White House counsel); David Gambrell, another Atlanta lawyer who Carter later named to fill a Senate vacancy created by the death of Richard B. Russell; Charles C. Barton, an Atlanta real estate developer; Jasper Dorsey, president of Southern Bell Telephone and Telegraph Company; Bert Lance; and J. Paul Austin, chairman of Coca-Cola Company.*

Most of those contributors, even in the pre-Watergate days of the late sixties and even for the populist of 1976, represented "special interests." And Jimmy Carter, from then to the presidency and beyond, enjoyed the political rewards that came from his contacts with the special-interest community, whether in Georgia or in the national arena. But because he was a Georgia politician those contacts assured almost immediate communication with a national and international ruling elite that would help propel him to the most powerful political position in the world.

It was much more a natural confluence of mutual interests that brought Carter and the ruling class together than any cabal or conspiracy hatched in the early years of the seventies. The small fry simply grew up and joined the

---

*Just after Carter won the presidential election New York *Times* reporter Nicholas Horrock discovered that Carter had one important contributor who had ceased being influential. In fact, Erwin David Rabhan, a close friend of Carter's who during the initial stages of the gubernatorial campaign had loaned his plane to Carter and eventually poured some eight thousand six hundred dollars into the campaign chest and who was also a house guest of Carter's at the governor's mansion for almost three weeks in 1974, was, according to Horrock, the "focal point of a wide-ranging federal investigation into alleged business fraud and accusations that money from organized crime was funneled into the business community" in Atlanta. But Rabhan had disappeared.

shoal. What did have to be planned was the hyperbolic presidential campaign to convince a ruling-class weary electorate that Jimmy Carter owed "the people everything" and "the special interests nothing."

It may have been just an accident that J. Paul Austin's name was on the list of large contributors to the Carter campaign for governor of Georgia in 1970. But seven years later, with Carter in the White House and Coca-Cola beneficiaries dancing about the red-carpeted corridors of political power, the Coke-connection seemed less than innocent and surely was more predestined than accidental. But whatever it was, there seemed little doubt that, as William Safire remarked some time later, "It's the real thing."

Coca-Cola was born in Atlanta almost forty years before Jimmy Carter was born near Plains. By the time the latter became president, still calling his home Plains, the former was one of the world's most powerful corporations, still calling Atlanta home.

Coca-Cola was the nation's sixty-ninth largest industrial corporation: its annual sales hovered just over three billion dollars; it was the world's largest consumer of granulated sugar—a million tons a year; had the world's largest privately owned truck fleet, biggest retail sales force and probably best-known product; and spent some two hundred million dollars a year on public relations alone. Its chairman, J. Paul Austin, flew in the rarefied atmosphere of influential executive boardrooms. He was chairman of the Rand Corporation (of which Zbigniew Brzezinski and James Schlesinger were associates), a trustee of the California Institute of Technology (of which Harold Brown was president), member of the Trilateral Commission (see pages 192–193), director of Morgan Guaranty Trust (of which Carter's Secretary of the Navy was also a director), a regent of the Smithsonian Institution, a director of General Electric, et cetera.

Not only did the company chairman provide seed money for Carter's second gubernatorial bid; Coke executives chipped in with campaign contributions while he was governor; the corporate aircraft whisked him around the country as he made his political contacts while ostensibly drumming up business for the state; and J. Paul Austin was there again to host a lucrative New York City fundraiser on behalf of the Carter presidential campaign.

There were less overt, if not more important, examples of mutual interests. When Coca-Cola testified before a congressional committee as a result of a 1971 Federal Trade Commission complaint against it, it brought legal counsel in the person of Joseph Califano (the same person President Carter chose to head HEW). When it needed legal advice in Atlanta it turned to King & Spalding (where Carter friend and presidential confidant Charles Kirbo, his attorney general Griffin Bell, and his transition team director Jack Watson could be found). When it wanted television commercials, it turned to New York advertiser Tony Schwartz (as did Carter during the presidential campaign).

It was odd: Jimmy Carter continually flattering the "two hundred fifteen million Americans," constantly telling them that his government would be as good and honest and competent as they were, promising them he was just as much an outsider as they were—and Jimmy Carter wheeling and dealing in the well-defined, tightly constrained, traditionally tiny circles of the jet-set of power-brokering. Both Jimmy Carter and the "people" may have been hooked on Coca-Cola. But the addictions resembled one another about as much as the horse resembled the cart.

The Carter administration was able to repay its debt to Coke a few months after taking control of the government. In May of 1977, because of plummeting world sugar prices which were threatening the existence of domestic producers unable to compete with the cheaper foreign imports, Carter decided to give the processors a government subsidy to keep them in operation. The real beneficiaries of the new policy, however, were the sugar users, who were saved from increased prices by the infusion of government money.

Instead of imposing a two-cent duty on imported sugar (one of Carter's options), which would have (a) added money to the Treasury, (b) raised the price of the imported sugar to a level which would have allowed domestic producers to compete, and (c) saved U.S. taxpayers an estimated two hundred forty million dollars a year in subsidies to the producers, the Carter administration opted for the two-penny dole which would have (a) taken money from the Treasury, (b) put an artificial lid on sugar prices, and (c) been of enormous benefit to the world's largest buyer of sugar, Coca-Cola (who had not, in any case, lowered the price of its soft drinks to reflect the falling price of sugar).

Then, in June, another interesting coincidence. Coke chairman Austin journeyed to Cuba for a meeting with Fidel Castro and, as William Safire wrote, "Upon his return . . . met in the White House with his friend, recent Coca-Cola stockholder Jimmy Carter."

Safire, who had a sensitive nose for potential high-powered conflicts-of-interest (which he soon used on the Bert Lance affair) tried to sniff out the reason for the Carter-Austin *tete a tete* but was rebuffed by spokesmen for both parties. So the columnist asked the pertinent questions in public. "Whom did Mr. Austin represent in his talk with Mr. Castro? Since Coca-Cola stockholders paid for the trip, and since Coca-Cola has a $27.5 million claim against Cuba for the confiscation of its properties in 1961, one would assume the Coke chairman went on behalf of the Coca-Cola Company.

"Why, then, the hush-hush briefing of the president immediately upon his return? . . . If this is an open administration, let's get some answers: What non-business matters did the Coke chairman discuss with Mr. Castro? What business-related matters did he discuss with Mr. Carter? Should a president send a campaign contributor with "personal greetings" to another chief of state when he knows it is a gambit for a business deal?

"The Carter-Coke-Castro sugar diplomacy is not merely a potential conflict of interest. It's the real thing."

By mid-July, even the chairman of the Senate Finance Committee, Russell Long (Democrat from Louisiana), was calling Carter's sugar policy the "Coca-Cola program." And on July twentieth Carter's own special trade negotiator Robert Strauss told the House Banking Committee that the subsidy program was "proving to be wholly ineffective," even adding that "it would not surprise me one bit if the Justice Department upheld" a ruling by the Comptroller General that the subsidy was illegal. But, Coke-22: the head of the Justice Department was a former member of one of Coca-Cola's law firms.

> "The test of a government is not how popular it is with the powerful and privileged few but how honestly and fairly it deals with the many who must depend upon it."
> —Jimmy Carter, Inaugural Address
> Atlanta, Georgia
> January 12, 1971

A little more than two weeks after the inaugural, on February 1, 1971, there was an entry in Jimmy Carter's appointment book for that Monday afternoon:

4:30 Gate House

5:00 Depart Executive Hangar—Lockheed

5:30 Mr. Robert Fuhrman. Lee Rogers (director of public relations at Lockheed Georgia Company)

7:30 Arrive Washington, Page Arriving National Airport, Reservations Washington Hilton.

On the next page of the book is the entry, "Mary [Beazley, Carter's appointments secretary]—Contact Earl Leonard at Coca-Cola 875-3411, ext 292 for Limousine Service from Airport to Hilton."

It seemed that Carter was beginning his term as governor enjoying considerable popularity with the powerful and privileged few: an aircraft put at his disposal by a giant multinational corporation (the state provided travel funds for official business and had both airplanes and trained pilots for gubernatorial trips); a limousine from Coca-Cola; a stay at the best hotel in town.

Lockheed Aircraft and Jimmy Carter got along quite well together during the four years that Carter was governor. The company had a large plant at Marietta, Georgia, where it built civilian and military aircraft, and as the nation's sixty-first largest industrial corporation (in 1976) its business tentacles reached worldwide (eventually prompting an international investigation into charges that it was bribing government officials as part of its techniques to augment its more than three billion dollars of annual sales). Lockheed bounded Carter around the world (as Coke did around the U.S.) and Jimmy reciprocated by selling the company's planes.

In April of 1972 Carter went for a three week tour through Central and South America ostensibly to promote the state of Georgia among Latin leaders. And it was Lockheed, then experiencing severe financial difficulties and hoping to stimulate its foreign sales, who provided the governor with a Jet Star executive plane for his travel.

Upon his return to Atlanta the governor dashed off an effusively friendly handwritten letter to Lockheed-Georgia Company's vice-president R. D. Roche which sounded more like a report from a company promotional executive and lobbyist than a populist politician:

Dear Bob,

One of the finest experiences of my life was being with you on the trip to Central and South America. In addition to the remarkable performance, luxury, and convenience of the Jet Star, the opportunity to learn more about Lockheed was extremely important to me.

It was obvious in my discussions with the leaders of the five nations—presidents, ministers of defense, and many others, that the C-130 Hercules is an airplane which is universally admired and appreciated. It was intriguing to see this great plane being used for coastal patrol, carrying troops and war material, bulldozers for the trans-Amazonic highway, cattle, building supplies, fish, civilian passengers, and trade seedlings. I have carried this message of admiration to our own national leaders in the State Department, Defense Department, and the Congress, and will continue to do so. In my opinion, our government and its agencies should marshal its efforts to help all of our friends throughout the world to buy and to use this plane because of its obvious quality and because it is such a fine example of a . . . contribution to both effective defense and peacetime usefulness.

I want to help in an active way and delayed writing to you until I could investigate ways to do so. The first step now, in addition to my public and private promotional efforts, should be for me to visit Lockheed and know at firsthand the problems and opportunities of your company. . . .

Again, all of us express our deep thanks to you and Lockheed.

Your friend, Jimmy

Carter had already experienced the "remarkable performance, luxury, and convenience of the Jet Star" the previous November, when Lockheed had flown the governor to New York for a visit with David Rockefeller.

His date book for November 23, 1971 read,

7:45 a.m. Arrive Dobbins AFB [Air Force Base near Atlanta] ¼ Dobbins Gate

8:00 a.m. Depart Lockheed Jet Star

10:00 Teterboro Airport, N.Y.

12:30 p.m. Lunch, Board of Directors Dining Room, The Chase Manhattan Bank, David Rockefeller

3:00 p.m. Depart Teterboro

5:00 p.m. Arrive Atlanta

Through the good offices of the chairman of Chase, Carter was able to make contact with other various and sundry representatives of east coast establishmentdom. Happily selling Lockheed aircraft and using the Coca-Cola company to set up meetings for him as he traveled abroad, Carter caught the eye of Rockefeller and one of his academic associates and consultants, Zbigniew Brzezinski, who were busy establishing a multinational think-tank called the Trilateral Commission. No one knew what Carter and Rockefeller spoke about while dining together in late 1971, but during 1972 Rockefeller, Brzezinski and former director of the Arms Control and Disarmament Agency, Gerard Smith, began casting about for Commission members to form their elite club. Members would represent the peerage among American, Japanese, and European businessmen, academics, politicians, and other "movers and shakers" as *Newsweek* called them. They were not going to meet for "abstract purposes," said the British journal *The Economist,* "they want to bring about action, and hence they want the new body to be a marriage of the intellectual and the influential."

And that it was. Only seventy-four Americans were chosen; and one of the two state governors picked to join the other "distinguished private citizens" was Jimmy Carter of Georgia. Brzezinski told British journalist Peter Pringle that "It was a close call between Carter and Reuben Askew of Florida, but we were impressed that Carter had opened up trade offices for the state of Georgia in Brussels and Tokyo. [Not so ironically, Carter's choice as the state representative in the Brussels office was a former Lockheed official.] That seemed to fit perfectly into the concept of the Trilateral."

In May of 1973 Carter officially (he had already been unofficially running for president for almost six months) joined and thus the gates opened wide for his entrance into the insiders circle. Carter's media consultant, Gerald Rafshoon, once admitted during the campaign that Carter's admission to the Trilateral was "one of the most fortunate accidents of the early campaign and critical to his building support where it counted." Among the movers and shakers on the Trilateral with Carter were Arthur R. Taylor, president of CBS; Leonard Woodcock, president of the United Automobile Workers; J. Paul Austin; Alden Clausen, president of the Bank of America; Hedley Donovan, editor-in-chief of Time, Inc.; David Packard, chairman of Hewlett-Packard Company; and I. W. Abel, president of the U.S. Steelworkers of America.

In the end, the Carter-Trilateral nexus served both the candidate and the commission: The former wanted to be president, and the latter wanted influence over policy. The relationship was best expressed by a trilateralist and one of Carter's campaign advisers, Samuel Huntington (whose "main claim to fame," as journalist Robert Scheer remarked, "is that he came up with the forced-urbanization program for Vietnam, which meant bombing the countryside to 'dry up the sea of people' around the Viet Cong."), who wrote that "To the extent that the U.S. was governed by anyone in the decades after World War II, it was governed by the president, acting with the support and cooperation of key individuals and groups in the executive office, the federal bureaucracy, Congress, and the more important businesses, banks, law firms, foundations and media, which constitute the private establishment."

It was anyone's guess as to whether Tolstoy or the Trilateral would sway Jimmy Carter more. But when the new president began assembling his co-rulers, the cabal theorists had a heyday. Not only did Carter's men share the paths of political and financial prestige, a disproportionate number of them came directly from the roster of David Rockefeller's commission. Members of the Trilateral Commission were:

Walter Mondale (Vice-President)

Zbigniew Brzezinski (Assistant to the President for National Security Affairs)

Cyrus Vance (Secretary of State)

Andrew Young (U.S. Ambassador to the United Nations)

Harold Brown (Secretary of Defense)

W. Michael Blumenthal (Secretary of the Treasury)

Anthony M. Solomon (Under Secretary of the Treasury for Monetary Affairs)

Richard N. Cooper (Under Secretary of State for Economic Affairs)

Warren Christopher (Deputy Secretary of State)

Richard Holbrooke (Assistant Secretary of State for East Asian and Pacific Affairs)

Paul Warnke (Director, U.S. Arms Control and Disarmament Agency)

Gerard C. Smith (U.S. Ambassador at Large for Non-Proliferation Matters)

Lucy Wilson Benson (Under Secretary of State for Security Assistance)

Elliot L. Richardson (U.S. Ambassador at Large)

Richard Gardner (U.S. Ambassador to Italy)

Robert R. Bowie (Deputy to the Director of Central Intelligence for National Intelligence)

> The story is told in Washington of two Senators. Senator A says "Carter is beginning to look like a one-term President." Senator B replies, "Yes, but when does it begin?"
>
> —New York *Times*, April 9, 1978

Most presidents seemed to prefer the fanfare of foreign travel to the headaches of domestic politics, and Jimmy Carter was no exception. He was having his share of presidential migraines as he packed his bags at the end of 1977 for a sixteen thousand mile jaunt to the far corners of the world which he hoped would help polish his tarnished image at home.

Hopefully he could leave behind the albatross of the Bert Lance affair which he had dragged around for so long. Perhaps Richard Helms and the deal negotiated with his Justice Department would be forgotten in his absence; or the fact that his "moral equivalent of war" energy bill still languished in Congress, where it had been for almost seven months. Maybe he could avoid the flak exploded by his retreat from his campaign promise to "never increase taxes for the working people of our country and the lower and middle-income groups," when he signed into law on December twenty-first a Social Security bill that meant tax increases of some two hundred twenty-seven billion dollars over the next decade. A foreign trip might distract attention from the fact that he had abandoned his campaign pledge to eliminate special tax treatment for capital gains; had not decreased unemployment; and had failed to make a dent in inflation—which jumped from a 4.8 percentage rate in 1976 to 6.8 percent during his first year in office.

A year-end summary of Carter's performance by the Washington *Post* indicated that the president had already reversed himself on a number of specific campaign pledges: making appointments to diplomatic posts exclusively on merit; reducing defense expenditures five to seven billion dollars annually; reducing foreign arms sales; reducing the number of federal agencies from one thousand nine hundred to two hundred; supporting the deregulation of new natural gas; removing the attorney general from political pressure by having a five to seven year term which would overlap the president's. A year-end poll by the opinion-research firm of Yankelovich, Skelly & White, Inc. conducted for *Time* magazine concluded that since March those with unfavorable impressions of Carter had jumped from 6 to almost 30 percent. "The two reasons mentioned most often," said *Time,* "were that Carter had not lived up to his promises and seems unable to get things done. These and other responses to the survey add up to disappointment that Carter is not a strong leader."

So it must have been with a certain amount of hopeful anticipation that the president announced at his first news conference upon his return from abroad, "It's nice to be back home, nice to start a new year."

It took less than thirty minutes, however, to start the year off in a direction that was anything but nice for Carter as he immediately embroiled himself in yet another "affair." He may have wished by the end of the news conference that he had stayed in New Delhi. In the short time that it took to answer five questions from reporters the president bumbled into another possible White House cover-up, as Carter first denied knowing anything about the dismissal of Philadelphia's Republican United States Attorney David Marston and then admitted that he had, in fact, asked his attorney general to "expedite" the matter after a call from a congressman that Marston was investigating. Carter's second year began in much the same way that the first had ended: confusion.

The Marston affair dragged on—not like Bert Lance, but long enough to rekindle and intensify the doubts about Carter's competence as president. If he could not handle the things immediately in his control—such as appointing U.S. attorneys—no wonder he was losing the perennially nagging battles against inflation and unemployment and taxes. His spring, 1978, inflation speech was billed as a major address but was greeted with remarks such as those of Michael Evans, president of Chase Econometric Associates: "President Carter's anti-inflation speech contained nothing new other than the appointment of Robert Strauss as a latter-day stand-in for King Canute" (an eleventh-century Danish king who ordered the ocean to retreat).

In late March it was Strauss, the former head of the Democratic National Committee, who called a secret meeting with Charles Kirbo, Griffin Bell and a few other Carter advisers to discuss . . . Jimmy Carter. The president was in "terrible shape politically," they concluded, and Kirbo was dispatched to inform the president, if he didn't already know. The New York *Times* was saying in public that it thought the "atmosphere now is turning sour. People who snickered whenever Jerry Ford bumped his head wonder whether Jimmy Carter has lost his."

The administration was on the defensive, trying mightily to shift the balance. There were staff reshufflings, cabinet meeting retreats at Camp David, presidential campaign-like tours around the country, tough talk for the Russians, and a new image-making machinery to let the people know of Carter's accomplishments. The mid-term elections were only a few months away, Carter would soon be half-way through his presidential term, it was a little late to talk about the "new" and "inexperienced" president and not too early to worry about the 1980 election. And with the polls still sagging, there was much to worry about.

By mid-July, 1978, Carter was ready for a major step in the campaign to regain public confidence when once again he came face to face with the differences between running for president and being president.

Off to Germany for an Economic Summit meeting with European leaders, Carter would have the opportunity to prove his strength among foreign leaders. At the same time the Russians were giving him the chance to regain some moral authority by deciding to stage a provocative trial of two famous dissidents: Anatoly Shcharansky and Aleksandr Ginzburg. His media adviser had scheduled him for an unusual prime-time television news conference upon his return as the first new effort to show the American people what their president was about.

But Carter was blind-sided by his own men. First, United Nations Ambassador Andrew Young was in Geneva telling a French socialist newspaper that the trial of Shcharansky was "a gesture of independence" by the Soviet Union that should have no real effect on the course of detente. "After all," said Young, "we also have hundreds, maybe thousands of people in our jails that I would call political prisoners." That remark humiliated Carter who was already under the gun from the hawks to show the Russians some U.S. muscle. Then came the disclosure that some of the bellicose senators who were accusing the administration (and this *before* Young spoke out) of "acquiescence that verges on complicity" in the trials were actually being egged on by members of Zbigniew Brzezinski's national security team.

While Carter was stewing in the boiling broth that his own advisers were pouring on him over Soviet dissidents, word came from Washington that presidential adviser Dr. Peter Bourne had become involved in a potential drug law violation. Not wanting to repeat the agony of another Bert Lance affair, Bourne resigned, but not without first admitting that there was a "high incidence" of marijuana use among members of the White House staff and an occasional use of cocaine.

That Friday evening, July twenty-first, the day that Bourne resigned, was not the best time for Carter to appear on prime-time television in front of a press that was ready to run him through the Bourne gauntlet. He disposed of the affair by simply saying he would be "glad to answer questions on other items." But it was an unsmiling and uncomfortably somber president who stood stone-faced for thirty minutes showing the obvious cracks of strain, stumbling over pronunciation of words, at one point saying that some business leaders have complied with our request; some labor leaders have required (sic) our request. . . ."

☆ ☆ ☆

President Carter, it seemed, kept bumping into Candidate Carter who kept running into Jimmy Carter who kept stepping on the toes of Outsider Carter who was constantly trying to cover up for Insider Carter who was continually compromising Moral Carter.

THE BERT LANCE AFFAIR: A SYNOPSIS

". . . to be perfectly frank," said the president on September 21, 1977, with possibly more candor than he realized, "the constant high publicity that has accrued to this case . . . creates doubt among the news media, among the people of this country about the integrity of our—of me and our government."

The doubts never completely disappeared. Months after he had symbolically washed his hands of the case by accepting Lance's resignation, Carter still heard calls for a special prosecutor and charges of obstruction of justice. Unlike most of the prominent Watergate figures who left public office in disgrace, each going his separate way (if only to different prisons), leaving Washington and national politics behind (except in book form), fading from public attention except as occasional (historical) reminders of the brooding of power-corrupted men, Bert Lance stayed in the arena of power, continuing to cultivate his friendship with the president.

The following pages are a skeletal summary of Lance's audacious rise and humiliating fall, and some of the powerful friends he made along the way.

A RAGS-TO-RICHES-TO-RESIGNATION CHRONOLOGY OF JIMMY CARTER'S FAVORITE "BANKTICIAN"

1951 Lance hired by his father-in-law as a teller at the Calhoun (Georgia) National Bank at ninety dollars a week.

1961 Lance becomes president of Calhoun National.

1965 Lance buys controlling stock of Calhoun National.

1970 December. Lance confirmed as Governor Jimmy Carter's head of the Georgia Highway Department.

1973 Winter. Lance announces candidacy for governor; discloses net worth of $3.4 million; finishes third in the Democratic primary.

1974   The Comptroller of the Currency begins
                          examination of Lance's Calhoun bank.
                          Governor Carter announces his candidacy for
                          president.

1975   Lance negotiates loan from Manufacturers
                          Hanover Trust in New York for $2.7 mil-
                          lion toward purchase of controlling stock
                          in National Bank of Georgia in Atlanta.

June.   Lance brings Carter to New York to meet Lew
                          Jenkins, one of MHT officers who handled
                          recent loan to Lance.

December.   The Comptroller of the Currency imposes an
                          enforcement agreement on Calhoun Bank
                          prohibiting questionable banking practices
                          such as large personal overdrafts by Lance.
                          Comptroller's office asks Justice Department
                          to investigate for possible fraud.

1976   Central States Teamsters deposit eighteen-
                          million-dollar pension fund in National
                          Bank of Georgia (NBG).
                          NBG gives Carter's Warehouse, Inc. a $2.4
                          million loan, double the normal line of
                          credit.
                          Calhoun Bank deposits two-hundred-
                          thousand-dollars (interest free) in First Na-
                          tional Bank of Chicago.

11/2   Carter wins presidential election.

11/22   Lance visits Donald Tarleton, head of Atlanta
                          office of Comptroller of Currency; the en-
                          forcement agreement against Calhoun
                          Bank rescinded the same day.

11/24   The New York *Times* reports in a front page

1976 (cont.)

story that Lance will be a Carter cabinet member.

12/1   Lance lawyer Sidney Smith calls the federal attorney in Atlanta.
Lance calls Carter in Plains; Carter recalled on 9/21/77 that Lance Justice Department investigation would be halted.

12/2   Justice Department calls off its investigation of Lance.

12/3   Carter nominates Lance as his chief of the Office of Management and Budget; says Lance will sell his $3.5 million interest in NBG, the fifth largest bank of the state.

1977   1/4   Carter administration ethics guidelines and conflict-of-interest standards released.

1/6   Lance borrows $3.4 million from First National Bank of Chicago to refinance loan from MHT; terms of the loan later reported to be very favorable.

1/20   Lance confirmed as head of OMB.

April   Alleged meeting between Lance and two men who want advice on assembling a purchasing group for Financial General Bankshares, Washington's second largest banking company.

7/6-7   Shares of NBG worth $8.50 ; down from $14.50 in January.

7/12   White House releases letter Carter sent to Senate Governmental Affairs Committee asking that the deadline requirement for sale of Lance NBG stock be lifted.

1977 (cont.)

7/21   "Carter's Broken Lance," New York Times column by William Safire; says Lance received "sweetheart loan" from Chicago bank.

7/22   Senate Committee to investigate the Lance loan.

7/25   "Boiling the Lance," Safire in NYT.

8/11   "Lancegate," Safire in NYT. Safire predicts that "belatedly aroused, the comptroller, the SEC, Senator Proxmire, and the press will all do their duty. Mr. Lance will resign and try to take the scandal out the door, while Mr. Carter professes to be above it all."

8/18   Comptroller of Currency issues partial report on Lance's past banking practices, mentioning some fifty irregularities.
Lance news conference; Carter joins him, expressing his complete support: "Bert, I'm proud of you."

8/23   Carter press conference; seven of twelve questions are about Lance.

9/8   "The Skunk at the Garden Party," Safire in NYT; calls for special prosecutor.

9/12   "Beyond Lance," Safire in NYT; charges that "Carter and his men have covered up wrongdoing and conspired to deceive the public."

9/13   Lance says, "I'm not going to quit and that means I'm not going to quit."

1977 (cont.)

9/14   Presidential press secretary Jody Powell apologizes to Senator Charles Percy for attempting to plant false and damaging story about the senator in various newspapers.

9/15-17   Lance's day in court: testifies before Senate Governmental Affairs Committee and a national television audience.

9/19   Justice Department sets up special panel to handle all Lance materials.

9/21   Lance quits.
Carter says he knew of the Comptroller and Justice Department investigations of Lance on December 1, 1976.
Lance indebtedness stands at over five-million-dollars.

9/22   Press secretary Powell says Carter did know of the Comptroller report on December 1, 1976, but not the Justice Department investigation.

9/29   The president says, "I don't recall at all ever knowing that the Justice Department itself was involved in the Bert Lance overdraft or other problems last year."

November/ Lance sells his NBG bank stock to Saudi Arabian for some four-dollars more a share
December   than he paid for it.
Lance goes to work for Pakistani banker who arranges to pay off Lance loan from First Chicago.
A Federal Grand jury empaneled in Atlanta to investigate Lance for possible criminal violations of the law.

1978	1/20	Carter appears with Lance at five-hundred-dollars-a-plate fundraiser in Atlanta. Lance retains his diplomatic passport and pass to the White House.
	2/10	The SEC begins investigation into a possible illegal takeover attempt of FGB.
	2/17	FGB files suit against Lance and a number of others for secretly conspiring to illegally acquire controlling stock.
	3/17	SEC files suit charging Lance and others with illegalities in takeover of FGB.
	3/22	White House announces that Lance turned in diplomatic passport earlier in the week.
	4/12	Lance addresses convention of American Society of Newspaper Editors: accuses press of "careless, erroneous or biased reporting" of his banking practices.
	4/18	William Safire wins a Pulitzer Prize in journalism for his columns on the Lance affair.
	4/26	The SEC and Comptroller of Currency file a ninety-page complaint against Lance accusing him of "fraud and deceit" and "unsafe and unsound banking practices" while a banker in Georgia. The White House says Carter's relationship with Lance is unchanged and he still carries special staff pass to enter.

THE CONNECTIONS OF BERT LANCE

J. Robert *Abboud:* Head of the First National Bank of Chicago; refinanced Lance's Manufacturers Hanover

Trust loan with personal loan of $3.4 million. A prominent Chicago Democrat and college roommate of John *Moore.*

Agha Hasan *Abedi:* Pakistan-born wealthy financier and head of London-based Bank of Credit and Commerce International (24 percent-owned by Bank of America. Hired *Lance* right after his resignation and paid off his loan to *Abboud.* Acted as go-between for *Lance* and *Pharaon* in purchase of NBG stock and contact for Mideast investors in FGB takeover. An associate of Jackson *Stephens* and co-defendant with *Lance* in the SEC civil suit.

Sheikh Kamal *Adham:* Former head of Saudi Arabian CIA; associate of *Abedi* and *Pharaon* and co-defendant with *Lance* in SEC suit.

Philip *Alston:* Head of prominent Atlanta law firm; on advisory board of Citizens and Southern Bank which loaned *Lance* over one-hundred-thousand-dollars for his gubernatorial campaign; appointed ambassador to Australia by *Carter.*

Griffin *Bell:* Attorney General; former federal circuit judge and law partner of Charles *Kirbo;* owns two-thousand shares in NBG; friend of *Lance* and boyhood chum of *Carter.*

Robert *Bloom:* Acting Comptroller of Currency prior to and during Lance confirmation hearings for OMB director; okayed termination of enforcement agreement with *Lance* bank and gave Senate a "no-violation" letter about *Lance,* later saying he didn't want to be "the skunk at the garden party." Resigned as Deputy Comptroller in early 1978; went to work for law firm of Eugene *Metzger.*

Michael *Blumenthal:* Secretary of the Treasury.

Jake and C.H. *Butcher:* Own banks in Knoxville and Nashville which gave loans to *Lance* of over four-hundred-forty-thousand-dollars; asked *Lance* to get them a meeting with *Blumenthal.*

Jimmy *Carter:* President; former governor of Georgia; part owner of Carter's Farms Inc. and Carter's Warehouse partnership which received a number of loans from NBG; good friend of *Lance* whom he appointed head of Georgia Highway Department in 1970 and Director of OMB in 1976.

Charles *Kirbo:* Atlanta lawyer; *Bell's* former senior law partner; confidant and good friend of *Carter.*

Eugene J. *Metzger:* Washington D.C. lawyer and counsel to FGB as well as major stockholder; co-defendant with *Lance* in SEC suit; his firm offered *Bloom* a job.

G. William *Middendorf:* President of Financial General Bankshares; former Secretary of the Navy; according to the SEC suit he met with *Lance* to discuss takeover of FGB while Lance was OMB director.

John *Moore: Carter's* "ethics" chief during the transition period; a member of the *Alston* law firm; *Abboud's* Harvard College roommate; appointed by *Carter* to head the Export-Import Bank.

Sheikh Zayed bin Sultan al-*Nahyan:* President of the United Arab Emirates and ruler of the oil-rich emirate of Abu Dhabi. An *Abedi* associate and co-defendant with *Lance* in SEC suit.

Ghaith R. *Pharaon:* Saudi millionaire and investor. Part of influential circle in Saudi Arabia that includes

Adham; an associate of *Abedi;* purchased *Lance's* NBG stock after introduction by *Abedi.*

Sidney *Smith:* The *Lance* lawyer who telephoned the U.S. Attorney in Atlanta the day before he closed a criminal investigation of *Lance;* member of *Alston* law firm.

Jackson *Stephens:* Wealthy Arkansas financier; member of Executive Committee of the Democratic National Committee and a major fundraiser; principal owner of Stephens Inc.; co-defendant with *Lance* in SEC suit; classmate of *Carter's* at Naval Academy and through *Lance* became *Carter* friend.

Donald *Tarleton:* Head of Atlanta office of Comptroller of Currency who rescinded enforcement agreement with *Lance* just after talking with him in November of 1976.

Index